Theobald Stein's statue of Ludvig Holberg, completed
in 1873 and placed at the entrance of the Royal Danish
Theatre in 1875.

Ludvig Holberg's Comedies

Gerald S. Argetsinger

Biographical Essay by
F. J. Billeskov Jansen
University of Copenhagen

Southern Illinois University Press
Carbondale and Edwardsville

Library of Congress Cataloging in Publication Data

Argetsinger, Gerald S., 1946–
Ludvig Holberg's comedies.

   Bibliography: p.
   Includes index.
   1. Holberg, Ludvig, baron, 1684–1754—Criticism
and interpretation. I. Title.
PT8090.A74   839.8'18409   82-5796
ISBN 0-8093-1058-9   AACR2

87 86 85 84 83   5 4 3 2 1

Rasmus Christiansen's conception of the interior of the Lille Grønnegade Theatre at the time of Holberg is the property of Teaterhistorisk Museum, The Royal Court Theatre, Copenhagen, Denmark, and is reproduced by permission of the Museum.

This book is for
John C. Argetsinger
(1915−1978)

Contents

Illustrations

Preface

Holberg's plays are about the only thing I never tire of reading.

—Henrik Ibsen

THE DANISH THEATRE was born on 23 September 1722. It was one of those rare instances in theatre history where a theatre did not evolve. Instead, it was consciously launched by a Frenchman as a business venture.

Even though Denmark had its own early dramatic presentations, these performances did not establish the groundwork for the Danish theatre. Liturgical drama, common throughout Catholic Europe, was performed during the Middle Ages. These serious and comic pieces were acted by clerics and by students in the grammar schools. The golden age of school drama, between about 1560 and 1630, saw student-acted performances flourish in Copenhagen and the provinces. But because of a stricter clergy, these plays almost disappeared by 1630.

Before the early eighteenth century, popular theatre in Denmark was performed by touring troupes from Holland, Germany, and even England. These foreign troupes brought their songs, dances, and plays to the outdoor fairs and streets of Copenhagen. At the same time, the royal

Danish court supported its own troupe of French actors, which performed the comedies of Molière and other light entertainments. But when the royal tastes changed to prefer bombastic German operas, the French actors found themselves on the street. Most returned to France—but not the troupe's leader, René Magnon de Montaigu. He enjoyed living in Copenhagen and wanted to stay, so he obtained permission to open a French theatre for the public. When that theatre failed, he decided to try something completely new—a popular Danish language theatre.

Confident that he would win approval, Montaigu petitioned the king for permission to produce plays in Danish. U. A. Holstein, the royal chancellor, and Frederik Rostgaard, chief secretary of the chancellery, were apparently responsible for making a Danish repertoire available. Some young justice clerks translated the popular Molière comedies and other light French entertainments. For original Danish comedies they turned to the man who recently had written a popular, satirical epic poem, *Peder Paars*. The man was Ludvig Holberg and he was to become the "Molière of the North," the "Father of Scandinavian Theatre."

The first Danish language production, on Wednesday, 23 September 1722, at the Lille Grønnegade Theatre, was a translation of Molière's *L'Avare*. The following Friday, 25 September, Ludvig Holberg's *The Political Tinker* opened. This, the first production of a Holberg play, was an immediate success. Six years later, in 1728, when King Christian VI closed the theatres in Denmark, twenty Holberg comedies had been produced and seven others written.

When the theatres closed, Holberg stopped writing

plays, but his comedies remained popular in written form. In 1746 the new king, Frederik V, allowed the theatres to reopen. Revivals of Holberg's comedies were again the mainstay of the Danish theatre. His seven previously unproduced plays were soon staged, along with six more comedies written for the new theatre. This brought the total of Holberg's dramatic writings to thirty-three comedies.

From that time until the present, the Royal Danish Theatre has been called "Holberg's Stage." His comedies have dominated the Danish repertoire for more than two hundred years. They have also been very popular in other Scandinavian countries. Indeed, since Holberg was born in Bergen, Norway, the Norwegians also claim him as their own great writer of comedies. Both the Danish and Norwegian national theatres have statues of Holberg overlooking their entrances. Today Holberg's comedies are as popular as ever in Scandinavia, both in printed and staged forms. There is always at least one Holberg comedy in the repertory of the Royal Danish Theatre.

It seems unusual that a playwright whose work is so popular in Scandinavia is almost unknown elsewhere. Holberg's plays have been performed successfully in other countries, mostly in the northern European nations such as Germany and Holland. But few of his scripts have been translated into English, and productions of them in America are rare.

The fact that Holberg's comedies have retained their popularity in Scandinavia demonstrates their theatrical effectiveness. Holberg is like many of the great comedy writers of the world; he relies upon the timeless appeals of situation comedy. The same things that made the eighteenth century Danes laugh, made the audiences of Menander, Molière, George S. Kaufman, and Neil Simon laugh.

Fifteen of the comedies have been translated into English. Unfortunately, these tend to be pedantic, rather than stageworthy, translations. They can be read and enjoyed, but new acting editions must be translated and made available to the English and American stages. Numerous excerpts have been translated for this book; they can also serve to introduce the uninitiated reader to the delights of Holberg's comedies.

Very little primary source material is available regarding the first productions of Holberg's comedies in the Lille Grønnegade Theatre. In fact, no records at all have been preserved from that theatre. The few speculations that are generally accepted are based upon the scripts. Complete records for properties, costumes, and scenery are available from the beginning of the Royal Danish Theatre in 1748. Since some of the original actors from the Grønnegade Theatre were recruited to stage plays in the new theatre, much can be inferred about the earlier theatre from the later one.

The edition of Holberg's comedies used for this study was the 1922 Commemorative Edition, *Comoedier og de Populære Skrifter (The Comedies and the Popular Writings)* in three volumes with introductions and commentary by Francis Bull, Georg Christensen, Carl Roos, S. W. P. Thomas, and A. Winsnes (Copenhagen: H. Aschehoug and Company, 1922). This particular edition provides both the standard texts of the scripts and all changes in the scripts since these were first published in 1731. It gives statistical information for each play's productions at the Royal Danish Theatre as well as information about foreign productions of each script. Notes and a glossary explaining the foreign and antiquated expressions in the plays are also provided.

Unless otherwise noted, all translations of Holberg's works or of Danish critical works were made by the author.

Acknowledgments

NOW THAT *Ludvig Holberg's Comedies* is finished and I think back over the seven years since I first began to study the man and his plays, I am amazed how many people had direct or indirect influence on my writing. Of those, there are some who need special thanks.

Roger Gross will always be first. He was the catalyst to my studies of Holberg, and he guided my original writing.

Per Pio and Jesper Jørgensen of the Royal Danish Library in Copenhagen provided invaluable guidance to my research.

Orson Scott Card made recommendations which guided me in adapting the scholarly manuscript into the book.

F. J. Billeskov Jansen of the University of Copenhagen, Department of Danish Literature, carefully read the first book manuscript and made important suggestions to amplify, clarify, and correct concepts and translations.

Warner Strong made the arrangements for the physical production of the final manuscript.

And my wife, Gail, was there through it all providing the strength and support to finish the project.

Ludvig Holberg

A Biographical Essay
by F. J. Billeskov Jansen

From 1380 to 1814 Denmark and Norway were united under the Danish crown. Ludvig Holberg, born on 3 December 1684, renewed Danish and Norwegian literature, but at the same time, by his endowments and background as well as his influence, became the *European* in Danish cultural life. To a great degree his life and activity were determined by the position of Europe in the period after the close of the Thirty Years' War in 1648. If we draw a circle around Holberg's dual fatherland about 1700, we find England as the land of revolt and liberty; a Spain shaken after the destruction of the "invincible armada"; a rich and powerful Holland. The literature of France was trend-setting, but the repeal of the Edict of Nantes manifested an intolerance that disquieted all of Europe's Protestants. The German Samuel Pufendorf described the constitution of his country as a monstrosity, and to bring order to the concepts he wove the incipient ideas of natural and international law into a systematic work, *De jure naturæ et gentium* (1672). Russia, with

Peter the Great's firm-handed reforms, was the land of surprises. When Denmark ceded the Scandia provinces to Sweden in 1658, Sweden gained access to the Kattegat. As a result of Denmark's defeat, the power of the Danish nobility was broken, and after 1660 the absolute monarchy increased the chances of making a bourgeois career.

The way for such a career had already been prepared in Holberg's family. Holberg was named after his mother's paternal grandfather, Ludvig Munthe, who was Bishop of Bergen; the family was well-situated. Holberg's father came of peasant stock; he entered Venetian war service, walked throughout the length and breadth of Italy, and in 1656 enrolled at the University of Siena. Holberg was proud of this father of his who had served his way up to lieutenant colonel. But his father died when Holberg, the youngest of twelve children, was a year old, and his mother died nine years later. The children were scattered. Holberg spent a while in Østland, Norway with his mother's cousin, Pastor Otto Munthe, but after that he lived in Bergen until 1702 with his mother's brother, Peder Lem, a merchant, whose bluff humor he much appreciated. At grammar school Holberg had a learned and enterprising principal, Søren Lintrup. When the school, along with most of the town, was burned down, Principal Lintrup hastily sent the year's graduating students off to Copenhagen, where Holberg entered the university that summer, six months short of his eighteenth birthday. Soon after attaining his majority he was assigned a plot of land as a modest inheritance. He took service as a tutor in the household of Pastor Weinwich in Voss, but this position gave him a distaste for both teaching and preaching, which the aging parish priest sometimes asked him to do. In the fall of 1703 he traveled via Bergen to Copenhagen, where in March 1704 he passed the philosophical examination, comprised of Greek, Latin, Hebrew, physics, geometry, arithmetic, geography, metaphysics, and ethics. In April of the same year he took the theological examination, which qualified him to apply for a clerical living when he reached the age of twenty-five. But Holberg was not yet twenty and was not disposed to a clerical career. He returned—for the last time—to his native town to take employment as a tutor with the suffragan bishop Niels Smed. But, he records in his memoirs, he felt as if condemned to working in the mines (*"ad metalla damnatus"*) and broke free. From reading Niels Smed's travel diary he had found a short-term goal: he was going to see Europe.

It was the first turning-point in Holberg's life when, in spite of his family's opposition, he sold his plot of land and other possessions and sailed off with only sixty rixdaler to Amsterdam, a bustling city of international standing that aroused his admiration but made inroads into his purse. He had counted on earning some money by teaching French and Italian to beginners, and on this trip he may have spent some time working as a language teacher in the house of a Russian nobleman. In his memoirs he admits that, while taking the waters in Aachen, he attempted to bilk the hotel, but was caught by the landlord. On borrowed money Holberg returned to Norway. In Kristiansand he stayed with his second cousin Otto Stoud, a curate, whose sister Sophia he calls very beautiful; perhaps his heart was smitten. Holberg earned money by giving private language lessons, but was determined to go to England. With an affluent comrade, Kristian Brix, he set forth in the spring of 1706. They went to Oxford and were granted admission to the university library, the Bodleian. A new phase in Holberg's life had begun; he wanted to be a writer of popular instructive works, and in 1708 he arrived in Copenhagen with the manuscript of a manual of European geography and recent history. To his chagrin, H. O. Pflug had published just such a work in 1707. So Holberg divided his book into two: in 1711 he published *Introduction to the History of the Principal Kingdoms of Europe down to These Times*, and in 1713 a geographical *Appendix* to the original volume, on Germany, England, and Holland. As he says himself, Holberg was an avid reader of newspapers, and his contemporary history partly builds on the current newspapers and gazettes. After a time of poverty in Copenhagen he was given a fresh chance: in 1708 he accompanied a son of Professor Poul Winding to Germany. After their return he became house-tutor for Admiral Frederik Giedde, but in August 1709 Winding obtained for him free lodgings in Borchs Kollegium. And then Holberg's future plans began to take final shape; he wanted to qualify himself for a post at the university by writing a firsthand historical work. He conceived a bold project: he would bring the history of Denmark up to date. Several historians had brought the story as far as 1580. In 1711 Holberg could announce that he had described the reigns of Christian IV, Frederik III, and Christian V. It was doubtless this achievement that gained him the Rosenkrantz Stipend, a scholarship of 120 rixdaler per annum for four years, and, on 29 January 1714, the king's promise of the first vacant professorship at the university. His career was now assured. Holberg drew his stipend, though the conditions stipulated that for three of the four years he should sojourn abroad. But then came the news that Iver Rosenkrantz, the patron of the scholarship, on the basis of Holberg's "promotion" had appointed a new recipient. The trustee of the scholarship, Professor Hans Bartholin, advised Holberg to travel abroad immediately. On 21 May Holberg wrote from Amsterdam that he would stay in France until a vacancy arose. He kept his scholarship.

It is ironic that Holberg was forced out on his great journey to France and Italy that so pervasively influenced his work and, in turn, Europe itself. He got to know the people everywhere he went, partly because a shortage of funds obliged him to travel and reside cheaply. In Paris Holberg visited the libraries and doubtless read mainly history. In the Mazarin library he saw students standing in line in the morning to secure Pierre Bayle's *Dictionnaire historique et critique* (1697), whose bold opinions on religion sowed doubts in many minds. But Holberg does not say that he lined up himself, and later he was unsuccessful when, at two Catholic libraries in Rome, he attempted to obtain Bayle's forbidden work for study. Holberg's curiosity had been aroused, but presumably he arrived home without being influenced by Bayle's doubts about the justice of God. The problem posed by Bayle did not become a live issue for Holberg until the 1730s. On the other hand, under the influence of Richard Simon, he did, before 1728, have some doubts about the Bible's divine origins. In Rome, where Holberg spent the winter of 1715/16, his taste for Italian baroque architecture and music was reinforced. In Paris he probably could not af-

ford to go to the theatre; in Rome he received strong impressions of the Italian masked comedy, the commedia
dell'arte, as a popular diversion. On his two-year journey
Holberg suffered much from malaria, but cured himself
by walking. Before he returned home in the summer of
1716 he had walked about two thousand kilometers along
the roads of Europe.

The years at Borchs Kollegium had been fruitful. Before Holberg set off on his travels he had composed a
Danish manual in a new science, without doubt encouraged by Christian Reitzer, a professor of law who lectured
on the law of nature and of nations. It was only a few
steps from Borchs Kollegium to Reitzer's residence, where
a large library was available to Holberg. Here Holberg
worked on his *Introduction to the Science of Natural
Law and the Law of Nations*, which was not published
until 1716, after his return from his travels. This system
of natural law, which Holberg adopted particularly from
Pufendorf, expresses a conception of human nature and
the structure of society that recurs throughout Holberg's
historical, literary, and philosophical writings: God has
endowed man with reason, a glorious light for grasping
and judging what good and evil are, if it is not warped by
bad upbringing and habits or by the passions that in no
small measure darken man's mind. In Pufendorf Holberg
also found Thomas Hobbes's doctrine of the strong royal
power that was necessary to protect one man against the
wickedness of another. Holberg's *Natural Law* is the best
introduction to his authorship and indeed to the century
of the Enlightenment itself. It became his best-selling
Danish book, reprinted in 1728, 1734, 1741, 1751, and
1763. After the law examination was introduced in 1736,

the book was read by most lawyers in Denmark and Norway. In the preface of 1716 Holberg had berated the university exercises, which were supposed to train the students in reasoning, but which, according to Holberg, trained them "to make black white and white black" by using "barbarous words and terms for which young people find a peculiar taste." By an irony of fate the professorship to which Holberg had to accede in December 1717 included metaphysics and logic, the two philosophical ancillary disciplines which he despised. In May 1720 he became professor eloquentiae, which meant he had to survey the classical Roman authors, including the satirists and comedy writers. This change coincided happily with his becoming a poet himself.

In Holberg's first works there was no inkling of the imaginative writer to come. But from 1719 we can see him emerging, in spurts like a dragonfly emerging from his chrysalis. The first stage was brought about by Holberg's choleric temperament. In the first part of his memoirs, 1728, he confessed of himself (in a passage that was omitted in the 1737 reprint) that he could not govern his envy when he heard laudatory remarks about competitors. When a dangerous and talented rival, Andreas Højer, in his *Dännemärckische Geschichte (History of Denmark*, 1718) permitted himself an offhandedly superior comment upon Holberg's *History of the Principal Kingdoms of Europe*, Holberg conceived a lifelong hatred of him. Under fictitious names Holberg composed two short Latin works in which he attacked Højer as a teacher of natural law and insinuates that as a polymath—jurist, physician, historian—he was something of a charlatan. In these vituperative works anger turned Holberg into a poet. Juvenal became an appropriate model when Holberg then tried his hand at a satire in Danish alexandrines, *The Poet Advises His Old Friend Jens Larsen Not to Marry*, in reality a rejection of the married estate, which probably still tempted the thirty-year-old Holberg.

In his next stage Holberg became aware of his comic imagination. In one of the illustrated editions of Boileau's *Œuvres*, he probably came across an engraving showing two groups of enraged clerics flinging books at each other: they were scrapping about the positioning of the lectern, *Le lutrin*, which was the title of Boileau's comic epic. It would seem that, in a flash of inspiration, Holberg pictured the disputatious professors and students at the University of Copenhagen. Nothing more came of it immediately, but soon Holberg made his great leap into the wide spaces of imagination. From his grammar school days, he knew Virgil's *Æneid* half by heart, but had no respect for the faithless Prince Aeneas. In Paul Scarron's *Le Virgile travesti* (1648) he had seen a burlesque retelling of the plot of the *Æneid*. So Holberg determined to tell the tale of a Danish Aeneas, a common shopkeeper, Peder Paars, who on a journey to Aarhus is shipwrecked on the island of Anholt in the Kattegat. Paars becomes ridiculous because, with thickheaded imperturbability, he accepts the blows of fate. The long alexandrine poem— 6,249 lines of verse—advances in powerful, almost primitively comic visions. When Holberg reached the third canto of the first book, he inserted, with a humorous preamble, the battle of the books at the university—it was not to be wasted! *Peder Paars*, which appeared in 1719, attracted attention and was reprinted. Anholt's owner, Frederik Rostgaard, complained to the king about this calumny on the island's population, but the king found the poem jocular and dismissed the protest.

There is no doubt that, after writing *Peder Paars*, Holberg felt himself to be a poet of note. A verse apologia, *Critique of Peder Paars* (1722), is a eulogy of poesy: "One with amazement reads, in Homer's book of gold / At the imagination, not at Greek wars of old." Poets win honor for their nations: Cervantes, Molière, Boileau, indeed Scarron. A great jurist provides learning, but a poet provides wit: "The one is wise and shrewd; the other is divine." So profound was Holberg's joy at his released poetic skill. *Four Mocking Poems* (1722) contained, besides this tribute to imagination and the Jens Larsen poem, two philosophical poems in which the contrasts in human nature (which *Natural Law* had clarified) are set over against each other. In *Apologia for the Singer Tigellius* it is maintained that we are all as fickle as this Roman artist; in *Democritus and Heraclitus* that mankind is to be both laughed at and wept over—though chiefly the former. Along with the mocking poems appeared *Zille Hansdotter's Defense of Womankind*, in which Holberg, as in his *Natural Law*, asserts the equality of woman with man.

Peder Paars and the mocking poems were published under the pseudonym Hans Mikkelsen; but the author was known, and it was not surprising that he was called upon to write comedies when the plan was to be realized for a theatre in Copenhagen. There was a firm theatre policy behind the project; it was backed by high officials U. A. Holstein and Frederik Rostgaard, and their intention was clearly to create a popular theatre. We can see this from the surviving translations: French verse comedies are rendered into Danish prose, and polished style is made more colloquial. Holberg followed this watchword in the twenty-five comedies he wrote from 1722 to 1726 for the Lille Grønnegade Theatre, which opened on 19 January 1722. During this ferment of creation Holberg found an outlet for his own comic imagination and at the same time drew upon old and freshly acquired knowledge of comedic literature from antiquity to his own time, including the plays of Molière and his followers that were being performed concurrently with Holberg's own. Holberg's plays appeared as three volumes, *Comedies* (1723–25), and were reprinted and expanded to five volumes as *The Danish Stage* (1731), to which a late harvest was added as volumes 6 and 7 in 1753–54. Holberg first vied with the great comedy of character of the Molière school; then returned, in a series of thrusts, to the Italian masked comedy, which he knew from the French editions of *Le théâtre italien* and *Le théâtre de la foire*; then moved gradually to themes from Roman antiquity; and finally, in his philosophical comedies of old age, dug right back to ancient Greek comedy. But at each stage Holberg shows his originality. In choice of subject, *The Political Tinker, Jean de France, Gert Westphaler, Erasmus Montanus* are original. The mighty comic oscillations of *Jeppe of the Hill* have their basis in an everyday realism that French comedy did not know; Molière has no counterpart to the character of Jeppe. *The Fickle Woman* has a forerunner, though not a model, in Destouches' *L'irrésolu* (1713). *Jacob von Tyboe* is a skillful localization of Plautus's *Miles Gloriosus*, as too *Don Ranudo* and *The Honourable Ambition* mark themselves out considerably from their common origin in Molière's *Le bourgeois gen-*

tilhomme. And when Holberg borrows the outline of Molière's *Le malade imaginaire* for *The Busy Man,* we see how Holberg carries the character-figure's bad quality to an extreme that Molière does not know. In Holberg's best figures there is an element of insanity, as in Cervantes' Don Quixote, who is the matrix for Holberg's fools. *The Maternity Room* is a comédie à tiroirs, a "drawer" comedy, in which a gallery of subordinate characters appears in series. It is after Molière's *Les fâcheux* and particularly his pupil Boursault's *Les fables d'Esope* (which was performed in Denmark) and *Le mercure galant.* Holberg uses the same method again in the last act of *The Fortunate Shipwreck.* The theme in *Journey to the Spring* is found in Molière, Regnard, and in the *Théâtre italien.* From the last source Holberg took numerous comic motifs and speech-lines. He felt akin to the Italians' devil-may-care comedy; this emerges from the comedies of parody *Ulysses von Ithacia* and *Melampe* and the drastic comedy of terror in *Without Head or Tail* and *Witchcraft.* The latter, particularly, is pure jest; it is, as it were, a wandering harlequinade paying a visit to Thisted, and it is a mistake to find traces of torture in it. It was particularly the Italians who provided Holberg with the fixed stock roles of the comedies of intrigue (Jeronimus, Leander and Leonora, Henrich and Pernille), which we meet in *The Christmas Room, Henrich and Pernille, The Invisible Ladies,* and *The Arabian Powder.* Holberg sets the scene of *Diderich—Terror of Mankind,* whose subject is taken from Plautus's *Pseudolus* and *Curculio,* in Venice. When Holberg wrote some new comedies for the theatre after its reopening in 1748, *Abracadabra* was a reworking of Plautus's *Mostellaria.* Two comedies placed abstractions on the stage: *Plutus* wealth, and *The Republic* the state, as in Aristophanes' *Plutus* and *The Knights*. In epistle 447 Holberg commends himself for having "renewed again the old Greek plays." Around the half-yearly settlement day on 11 June the theatre demanded and was given topical plays whose horseplay might amuse out-of-town visitors to the capital: *The Eleventh of June* and *The Peasant Boy in Pawn*. The former was inspired by Molière's *Monsieur de Pourceaugnac*, the latter by a comedy in the *Théâtre italien*, *Le banqueroutier*. Holberg made both farces redolent of Copenhagen taverns and hostelries. In Holberg's comedies rearises the European comedy tradition, apart from the English (Holberg did not know Shakespeare); instead of the Spanish comedy tradition in drama (Lope de Vega, Calderón), we find the enormous impact of Cervantes' novel.

In the thick of his busy comedy writing, Holberg took leave of absence from the university in 1725–26, officially to take the waters at Aachen, actually to see plays in Paris. It grieved him that, on the closing of the Grønnegade Theatre on 25 February 1727, he had to write *The Burial of Danish Comedy*. However, the plays continued into 1728, when the Copenhagen fire of 20–22 February stopped all amusements. In 1730 Frederik IV died, and Christian VI called the theatre the work of the devil. But by then Holberg's poetic frenzy had worked itself out. He bade farewell to Danish poetry with a singular series of poems, *Metamorphosis* (1726), in well-turned alexandrines and short verses. And he wrote the postscript to the period in the form of the first installment of his life's romance, *Epistola ad virum perillus-*

trem (1728), memoirs set out as a letter to an undoubtedly fictitious man of renown. It is a sprightly account, particularly of the travels of his youth, a frank self-portrait as well as an unfeigned advertisement of his own works. To tempt translators he outlines the plots of the comedies hitherto printed, but only gives the titles of the unprinted ones.

After his poetic frenzy, Holberg was seized by a historical one. Before his poetic activity he had had a plan for a *Description of Denmark and Norway*, which was now to be realized. This large work, published in 1729, was more or less intended to be a counterpart to Edward Chamberlayne's *Present State of England* (1678–81). Holberg was influenced by the Englishman's chapter divisions, buoyant presentation, and poetic quotations and anecdotes. But Holberg gives each chapter—on national character, form of government, religion, and so forth—a more thorough historical perspective. It is surprising, though, that he inserted his old unprinted account of the history of the three latest kings, hinting that he would like to have continued with that of the present monarch, Frederik IV: "But as His Majesty has most graciously assigned to others the composition of such a history, I shall conclude this chapter with the death of Christian V." Holberg wanted to show that *he* ought to have been the royal historiographer, and not Højer, who had been so appointed in 1722. This huge chapter was omitted when a new edition of the work appeared in 1749 under the title *The Spiritual and Secular State Denmark and Norway*. And by then Holberg had long since composed a complete and well-related *History of the Kingdom of Denmark* in three parts which concluded with Frederik III's death, when Dano-Norwegian absolutism, so life-giving to Holberg, had been assured. As a stimulating model he took the multi-volume *Histoire d'Angleterre* (1724) by Rapin de Thoyras, a French jurist who, because of his faith, had emigrated to England. With greater thoroughness than the Frenchman, Holberg, at the death of a king, gives an overall evaluation of his character and deeds. The psychological scheme and the ethical norm are the same as in Holberg's *Natural Law*.

In 1730 Holberg was appointed to the professorship of history, and when in 1732 history was made an examination subject at the university, he worked out two short textbooks, *Synopsis historiae universalis* and *Compendium geographicum*, both printed in 1733. *General Church History* (1738) and *Jewish History* (1742) combine sober appraisals of popes and prophets with religious emotion about historical figures like Luther and Moses. Holberg opens the first book with a brilliant history of Jesus Christ and closes the second with an observation upon the amazing preservation of the Jewish people through the ages: in their destiny we must "recognize the finger of God." Holberg moved into the field of biography with his *Comparative Histories of Heroes* (1739) corresponding *Comparative Histories of Heroines* (1745). Most interesting are the history of Peter the Great, who singlehandedly reshaped a whole empire, and the attempt to fathom an enigmatic woman like Queen Christina of Sweden.

During this impressive historical production, Holberg's third frenzy, the philosophical one, was preparing. In 1737 he continued his memoirs with *Epistola secunda* and in 1743 with *Epistola tertia*, to which he appended six practical, philosophical essays. He translated these into *Moral Thoughts* (1744), which contained his most finely pointed prose, influenced by Seneca and Montaigne. In the Latin romance *Nicolai Klimii iter subterraneum (Niels Klim's Underground Journey*, 1741), Holberg had anonymously battled against religious intolerance. In *Moral Thoughts*, his main philosophical work, he asserted man's right and duty to think for himself in all matters, including religion. We can trace Holberg's own development from the 1730s when his eyes were opened to Bayle's accusations against God. After models by the Roman Martial, the Englishman John Owen, and the Dane Henrik Harder, Holberg published a collection of Latin *Epigrammata* in 1737 and added to them in 1743 and 1749. They include a variety of moods: humorous, satirical, wanton, and edifying. Against Bayle, who made God responsible for the evil in the world, Holberg in 1737 objected, with Leibniz, that good cannot exist without evil (Epigram II, 94 and III, 78). In *Moral Thoughts* he is still on Leibniz's side against Bayle. But later the picture changes. Two volumes of Holberg's *Epistles* appeared in 1748, two more in 1750, and a posthumous one in 1754. In the first volume Holberg admits that Bayle's opponents have not solved the problem of the origin of evil, and in the next two he capitulates, taking refuge in the revealed doctrine of the Fall. (Among *Moral Fables* [1750], published at the same time, we meet a kindred pessimism in no. 81, a fascinating fable about the problem of evil.)

The epistles are philosophical commentaries upon the manifold reading of the aging Holberg. They deal with many subjects and are held together by an unshakably sound common sense. It was Holberg's opinion that the light of reason can guide us, but that our desires often give rise to incomprehensible conduct. For example, in Bayle's *Dictionnaire* Holberg read of Hipparchia, a Greek gentlewoman who married a Cynic, or dog-philosopher, who lived in poverty and filth. This reminded Holberg of a Danish noblewoman who found satisfaction in marriage only with a gross man of the lowest station. Thus two examples, Hipparchia and Marie Grubbe, become matter for an epistle, no. 89, on the corrupt taste of certain human beings. One of the last epistles, no. 447, carries Holberg's autobiography down to 1753.

After 1727 Holberg lost the desire to travel abroad, and he settled down like the cats he had mentioned in the preface to *Metamorphosis*. In 1737 he became university quaestor—i.e., bursar. As new archival finds have now confirmed, he was a zealous steward of university funds until he resigned the office in 1751. For Holberg had a feeling for private and public thrift. He had written a couple of Latin pamphlets in favor of the capital's exceptional economic status (1729) and of the East India Company (1728). Holberg's housekeeping was always modest; from 1740 he had an official residence on the corner of Fiolstræde and Kannikestræde in Copenhagen. From around 1730 he was earning good money from his authorship; he invested his savings in houses in Copenhagen, but when their prices fell, he bought landed estates. In 1740 he bought the estate of Brorup near Slagelse, and in 1745 added Tersløsegaard near Sorø. He had already made public in 1735 that he wished to bequeath his assets to the furthering of the Danish language. In 1747, on request, he destined his fortune to the Sorø Knightly Academy, which was intended to be a higher educational establishment for future officials. Its emphasis was on the teaching of natural and state law, recent history, and living languages. At the same time Holberg had his estates compounded into the Barony of Holberg. It was a satisfaction to him that he had become a baron on his own merits. As the yield on Holberg's capital was required for the running of the academy, on 1 May 1751 he made this fund over and continued his spartan way of life. As the senior professor at the university he was exempted from teaching; he spent his last summers at Tersløsegaard (which is now a Holberg museum). Like Voltaire, Holberg made a fortune by his pen, bought estates, and acquired the reputation of being a wise and humane lord of the manor. When the dreaded cattle disease which was scourging Europe reached Holberg's estate, he called together his tenants, and in everyone's interests, gave them the same advice that was printed in his *Reflections on the Cattle Disease Now Prevailing* (1746). Holberg and Voltaire were both authors and landowners of the Enlightenment. Ludvig Holberg died in Copenhagen on 28 January 1754 and was taken to the Cloister Church in Sorø, where he rests in a beautiful sarcophagus by Johannes Wiedewelt.

Holberg never married, and his touchy temper hardly permitted him intimate friends. But he was sincere when he returned to Danish society what he had earned from his books. When these works, undoubtedly without remuneration, were disseminated in other languages, he repaid to the circle of countries that defined his horizon what they had given him. In his century, Holberg was not only a Scandinavian, but a European author. Practically all his historical writings were translated into German, several also into Dutch. His *Natural Law* appeared in German; *Moral Thoughts* in German, Dutch, and French; the *Epistles* in German and Dutch; *Moral Fables* in German and Russian. *Peder Paars* was rendered into German verse, and from that into Dutch prose. With his plays, Holberg became the favorite comedy writer of German theater troupes. There are numerous editions of them in Dutch. *Niels Klim* was briskly translated before the end of the century into German, Dutch, French, English, Russian, and Hungarian. With *Niels Klim* Holberg was participating in a European struggle against intellectual coercion, in line with Montesquieu, for example; in epistle 520 Holberg translated a stirring passage on the Inquisition from *L'Esprit des lois*. And when, in the same work, he found aspersions cast upon absolutism, he published, four months before his death, in his highly personal French, a little book that was not without impact, thanks to Holberg's superior historical knowledge, *Remarques sur quelques positions qui se trouvent dans "L'Esprit des loix" par M. le baron de Holberg*. The wise old man's ready mind did not fail him when he entered into a debate with one of Europe's most penetrating intellects.

Ludvig Holberg's Comedies

ONE

Ludvig Holberg's Background

LUDVIG HOLBERG did not originally set out to be a playwright. In fact, he first began writing plays on request at the age of thirty-eight. He did not have a theatre background, in the sense that Shakespeare and Molière did; they virtually spent their lives in the theatre. Because of the absence of any indication of theatre activity, it is unknown to what, if any, extent Holberg actually attended the theatre before he began writing for the stage.

Holberg was not exclusively dedicated to drama. When there was a theatre available to produce his scripts, he wrote plays. When no theatre was available, he wrote poems, histories, fables, or in whatever literary form seemed apropos to the message he wished to communicate. Indeed, his thirty-three playscripts represent only about one-fourth of his collected works. Holberg's philosophical development cannot be traced in his plays as Ibsen's or O'Neill's can in theirs. No change in political, ethical, or religious attitudes is reflected in his scripts. In fact, Holberg wrote his first twenty-seven comedies during the six-year life of the Lille Grønnegade Theatre in Copenhagen. His final seven plays were written, almost as quickly, eighteen years later when the Copenhagen theatres were reopened. Even though Holberg was not a "theatre man," and even though his plays represent only one-quarter of his literary output, his literary reputation is based principally upon these comedies. Because of their popularity, Holberg has become known as the "Father of Scandinavian Theatre" and the "Molière of the North."

While Holberg began writing plays on very short notice, the study of his comedies and his notes regarding them indicate that he had definite opinions about playwriting. Three major influences on Holberg's writing were his own life and writing before 1722, the theatre traditions already established in Copenhagen, and the philosophical and dramatic writings with which Holberg was familiar.

HOLBERG'S EARLY LIFE AND WRITINGS

Ludvig Holberg was born on 3 December 1684, in Bergen, Norway. His father, Lieutenant Colonel Christian Nielsen Holberg, died two years later on 29 March 1686. At age ten, young Ludvig entered the Bergen Cathedral School for his primary education. The next year, 1695, his mother died in an epidemic. During his teenage years, Ludvig lived with his mother's cousin, Otto Munthe, parish priest in Fron, Gudbrandsdalen, Norway, and with his maternal uncle, Peder Lem, a merchant in Bergen.

In July 1702, at age eighteen, Holberg entered the University of Copenhagen. In less than two years, on 10 March 1704, he passed the philosophical examination (metaphysics, ethics, etc.); in April of the same year he passed the theological examination. Since passing these two examinations completed the Danish university education, Holberg returned to Bergen where he tutored in the home of the deputy bishop, Niels Smed.

In the early eighteenth century, Denmark and Norway (more one country than two) had not yet developed their own identities. Aristocrats followed the French modes. They adopted the French fashions, mannerisms, and activities, and even preferred to speak French to one another. The academicians taught classical philosophy in the classical languages. They were closed to new ways of thinking and rejected the progressive ideas being discussed throughout the rest of Europe. Theological instruction was given in the state religion, Lutheranism. The academicians also considered the Danish language inferior, contending that no important or deep thoughts could be communicated adequately in the common tongue.

Holberg quickly became discontented with Bergen and longed for the comparative intellectual stimulation of Copenhagen. He was also inspired to travel throughout Europe by reading Niels Smed's private travel diary. Holberg was only twenty years old and had completed his formal education, but he was eager to learn and experience anything new. So, he set out to further his education through travel.

This yearning for travel and experience was not new to Scandinavian youth. Others who had become discontented had ventured out, but had often elected to settle in the cities they visited, rather than return to their own "backward" homeland. Holberg was different. He may have been dissatisfied with some of the attitudes and conditions in Denmark, but Copenhagen was the city he called home. He decided that he would do his best to bring the Danes the good things of life from outside their own country.

Holberg spent nearly a year in Holland between 1704 and 1705, but in his whimsical autobiography he writes only anecdotes about how poor he was. It is not known whom he visited, what he did, or exactly how long he was there. He had no intention to spend his time studying; instead he ardently read the newspapers and steeped himself in Dutch culture. After returning from Holland, he spent six months in Kristiansand tutoring in French and English. Holberg also spoke German, Dutch, and Italian and could at least read and write Greek and Latin.

During the spring of 1706, Holberg sailed for England with Kristian Brix, a friend who was a graduate in theology. This time Holberg traveled to study. He spent much of his time reading scholarly books in the excellent Oxford library. He also became very friendly with the Oxford students and learned much from them about the Oxford system of education and English life in general. During the more than two years he spent in England between 1706 and 1708, Holberg developed much of the philosophy of education that would guide his own academic career in Copenhagen. In Denmark students studied a broad range of topics in a general manner; at Oxford students focused on limited topics, penetrating more deeply into areas of concern. In Denmark all students were taught to dispute in Latin; at Oxford little attention was given to the art of disputing and the standard of Latin was low. Holberg noted that at Oxford great respect was paid to authority and rules, with even the slightest error being immediately corrected. It was also in England that Holberg determined that his future lay in writing.

Holberg returned to Copenhagen during the summer of 1708. Here he spent time renewing acquaintances and talking about education and the style of life he had observed in England. His travels were teaching him that there were people in Europe who took pride in their countries and in writing in their own languages. He discovered that scholars outside Scandinavia freely discussed new thoughts and philosophies, new art forms and literature. While most of the Danish scholars to whom Holberg talked were unimpressed, a few were interested in the ideas Holberg was developing. Professor Poul Winding gave Holberg a stipend to travel to Dresden as a mentor for his son. So Holberg left Denmark for the third time in the fall of 1708. From Dresden, Holberg traveled to Leipzig, the intellectual center of Germany, and then to Halle, intent upon seeing the German philosopher Thomasius. Holberg later complained that the philosopher would talk only about the weather.

In January 1709, Holberg returned to Copenhagen, where he remained for five years. He had spent about one year in Holland, two years in England, and a few months in Germany. Although it is known that Holberg's travels introduced him to new ways of thought, new literature, and new cultures, little is known about the actual books he read or the people with whom he met and talked. When referring to these travels in his epistles, Holberg is always vague and whimsical. He apparently remembered them as a humorous time in which a young Scandinavian matured in the ways of the world. It is also known that he had very little money and could not spend much time at entertainments. In none of Holberg's writings is it recorded that he ever attended the theatre or studied dramatic literature in any way during these three journeys abroad.

During his five-year stay in Copenhagen, 1709–14, Holberg became a resident at a college, Borchs Kollegium. The residency also included a scholarship. Here, Holberg became very active in historical research and writing. During this time his first book, *Introduction to the History of the Principal Kingdoms of Europe*, was published. It was also during this time that Holberg embraced the philosophy that would become the undercurrent of all of his writings. The concept of "the rights of nature and of people" had become established throughout much of Europe during the seventeenth century. It was probably Christian Reitzer, a professor of law who lectured on the subject at the University of Copenhagen, who encouraged Holberg to write about the concept in Danish. The philosophy was based upon the writings of such men as Hugo Grotius, *De jure belli et pacis*, (*On the Responsibilities of War and Peace*, 1625), and Samuel Pufendorf, *De jure naturae et gentium* (*On the Rights of People and of Nature*, 1672) and *De officio hominis et civis* (*The Duties of Men and Governments*, 1673). Its basic thesis proclaimed that man does have a conscience which tells him what is right and wrong. Man does not, therefore, need to be told by others what is right and wrong. If people would simply use their own common sense, they could understand their shortcomings and improve their own lives.

To Holberg, these ideas came to provide a systematic understanding of the world that neither his religion nor metaphysics had provided. They gave new meaning to his basic Lutheran beliefs and clarified various points of view. Much of his writing was to communicate these ideas to his countrymen. For example, his entire library of character comedies was written to demonstrate various human shortcomings, with the hope of inciting his audience to overcome such faults and improve their own lives. He believed that a man did not have to resign himself to his imperfections, but that he could improve. That this belief became the foundation for Holberg's writings is also evidenced by the fact that when he wrote and had published in Danish the *Introduction to the Science of Natural Law and the Law of Nations* (finished in 1714, published in 1716), he had not added any new thoughts of his own. Holberg's Danish introduction to this school of thought is now hailed as Scandinavia's door into the Age of Understanding. It was absorbed into the Scandinavian point of view and became very important in the lives of Danes and Norwegians.

Holberg was also learning how to advance his own position. He wrote a history of the reigns of the Danish kings Frederik III and Christian IV and sent the manuscript to the reigning king, Frederik IV. About 1714, Holberg also petitioned the king for a professorship at the University at Copenhagen. On 29 January 1714, he was appointed a professor and was promised a position at the university as soon as there was a vacancy.

To sustain him until a position opened, Iver Rosen-krantz gave Holberg an important stipend to travel. In the spring of 1714, Holberg left on his fourth trip abroad. He was now thirty years old and had acquired a reputation as a historian. Again, Holberg makes no reference to attending the theatre or to reading dramatic literature. Since he spent some time in Paris, scholars have speculated that he must have seen some of Molière's plays, but the scholarly consensus is that he did not attend the theatre. Even with his stipend, he could ill afford such luxuries.

While in Paris, several of Holberg's friends tried to convert him to the French national religion, Catholicism. Other traveling scholars from Protestant countries had been joining the "Mother Church," including the famous Danish anatomist Jacob Winsløw. The pressure was so great upon Holberg that he became very set in the Danish Lutheran religion. His Lutheran beliefs, along with his belief in common sense and self-improvement, are manifest throughout his writings.

On this same journey Holberg visited Rome. He writes in his memoirs that there were ten to twelve commedia dell'arte troupes in Rome during the latter part of his stay and that one of them was lodged in the same place he was. He comments only that they annoyed him and that they performed one play, about a doctor similar to the one in Molière's *Le médecin malgré lui*. Holberg clearly developed a deep knowledge of both Molière's plays and the commedia dell'arte, but his writings give almost no indication of how he acquired it. Later in his life, Holberg tended to write about the plays he saw and the scripts he read, but the primary source material regarding his contact with the theatre or playscripts until after the time he began writing plays is limited to this one remark about the commedia dell'arte players in Rome.

During this fourth trip Holberg contracted malaria and spent most of his time recovering. He did most of his traveling on foot, not only because he was poor, but because he found that exercise improved his health. He went from place to place studying philosophies, books, and the people around him. Two years later, in 1716, Holberg again returned to Copenhagen.

Holberg's *Natural Law* had been printed while he was abroad. Now he wrote a new introduction tracing the philosophy's history. It also adeptly outlined a program in modern studies. Holberg placed man's moral development as most important; then he ranked the usefulness of the sciences, with medicine first, mathematics (including mechanics) second, and historical inquiry third. He felt that language studies were overemphasized. But worst of all was metaphysics, with its logic exercises and its system of abstract concepts.

The long-awaited vacancy at the University of Copenhagen came in December 1717—in the very area which Holberg least respected, metaphysics. Following the custom of the time, Holberg was required to present a formal, ceremonious laudation of metaphysics at his induction to the post. He filled his acceptance speech with irony and later referred to it himself as a funeral oration.

By 1719 Holberg had not yet tried his hand at poetry, fiction, or satire. He burst into his satirical writings, first in Latin and then in Danish, when he felt his ability as a scholar had been slighted. Andreas Højer, who had completed his education in medicine, history, and law at

Halle, was attempting to establish a career for himself in Copenhagen. His early writings on Danish history and on marriage between cousins had been severely criticized by the highest authorities. Holberg was personally outraged by Højer's preface to his history of Denmark. In this preface, Højer explained that he had derived no profit at all from Holberg's history, saying it merely followed Pufendorf. But Holberg was very proud of the original scholarship in his chapter on Denmark, which had built on the foundation of the earlier Danish historians Saxo and Huitfelt. Holberg became so angry that he published two anonymous polemics against Højer, satires which were very well received by both the students and the faculty at the university. Holberg was pleased not only by their acceptance, but also at the ease with which he had been able to write them. The style was natural to him.

The result of this popularity was that Holberg decided to write a satire directed at the university, feeling that perhaps this was the way to reach his colleagues with his cause. As he worked on the project, the idea grew and finally took the form of an epic poem. *Peder Paars* is chiefly a scholarly burlesque of the absurdity of typical scholarly disputations. In mock seriousness it deals with the question, "During the Trojan War, was Venus wounded in the right hand, the left arm, or the thigh?" The story takes place on a distant island called Anholt, where the inhabitants of the island are purposefully kept ignorant. The clergyman is arrogant. Government officials are slandered through the character of an ignorant bailiff. And university professors, against whom the satire is most heavily directed, are lampooned in the person of pedants who dispute the location of Venus's wound. Interestingly, in writing *Peder Paars*, Holberg created several of the character types who would become central figures in his comedies.

When the first episode of the poem was published in 1719 under the pseudonym Hans Mikkelsen, it caused an incredible commotion. Professor Hans Gram and Frederik Rostgaard, owner of the real Anholt, petitioned the king to have the book burned. They claimed that it made slanderous attacks on the university, the bishop, the magistrates, the professors, and the very word of God. They demanded that the anonymous author be found (probably knowing it to be Holberg) and punished. But King Frederik IV had a good sense of humor and dismissed the charges. Almost immediately, in 1720, Holberg was raised in rank by being appointed professor of Latin literature. The king's dismissal of the charges, and the promotion, seemed to give Holberg new boldness. Within the next year three more episodes of *Peder Paars* were published. There had never been such a successful book in Denmark. Within eighteen months three editions of the complete poem were sold out.

Along with his scholarly work at the university, Holberg continued to write satires. In 1722 he published in one volume the four *Peder Paars* episodes, goodnatured justifications of them, and *Zille Hansdotter's Defense of Womankind*, a humorous work which called for the liberation of women.

And so the development of Holberg's beliefs, ambitions, and satirical writings has been traced to the year in which he was to begin writing his comedies. In 1898, one

Holberg scholar, Edvard Brandes, writes so energetically about these developments that his lauding becomes humorous. Even so, his sentiments indicate the general attitudes toward Holberg in later times:

> He did not travel to become less Danish. Holberg never considered settling in any other country. He left only to harvest what the world had to offer. He brought back insights and ideas to the insipid students, the ringing of the mother tongue to the mute and Latin speaking (educators), nationalism to a subdued populace, and popular writings for a country without literature. That one man created a reading public and a nationalistic pride.
>
> . . . In his travels he learned to "reason"; nowadays we call it thinking for ourselves. He was criticized as having polarized the people and their language; now we say he helped to create a common pride and a way of thought.
>
> . . . He was the fresh wind that startled the sleepers to their senses. He caused them to jump up and run amuck crying, "To arms!" And he finally turned them away from their muddied thoughts.
>
> . . . The educators rose up against him. They were used to a doctrine which had nothing to do with reality, in a science which had no practical application.
>
> . . . But Holberg was unable to reach the educated. He had only castigated them. He was ready to try to reach the uneducated. He saw only one way to reach them—the theatre. He could not be held back. He had several comedies written by the time the Danish theatre opened.
>
> . . . The effect of the comedies was instantaneous and great. The audience poured in . . . and Holberg took them by the tail. He had awakened them.[1]

Holberg was a brilliant young man who was not sat-isfied to remain stagnant in northern Denmark while the rest of Europe was moving forward with national pride and with new art forms, ideas, and philosophies. He wanted the people to break out of their ignorance, and he wanted the academic leaders to lead the way by ridding themselves of their outdated traditions. At a time when it was acceptable to write scholarly works only in Latin, Holberg led the way by publishing his books in Danish. He showed that important ideas could be expressed in the vernacular and that the Danish language was suitable for clever and witty satires. Even though academia was against him, even though they railed against his appoint-ment and his satirical writings, the reading public and students rallied by buying, reading, and discussing his works.[2]

THE DANISH THEATRE AT THE TIME OF HOLBERG

Holberg's playscripts reflect the fact that he had ei-ther a conscious or an intuitive understanding of the the-atre before he began writing plays. It is also evident that he knew the current theatre conventions popular in Den-mark and was able to construct his plays with them in mind. So, it is important to briefly examine the theatre for which Holberg was about to write.[3]

As in other European countries, Denmark's drama dates back to the mystery and morality plays of the Mid-dle Ages. Vulgar farces appeared coeval with the morality plays. The morality plays had their origin in the church, with the depiction of Bible stories and the preaching of moral lessons, while the vulgar farces originated in the Shrovetide carnivals which led the way into Lent. During the 1500s the morality plays became mildly popular outside the church and were performed in the public squares and in the homes of the aristocracy. When the plays left the churches, the clergy took a smaller and smaller part in their production.

Having grown accustomed to allowing plays in public places, Denmark was prepared to accept foreign professional acting troupes. These first appeared in Denmark, from England, during the 1580s. English actors performed their music, dances, and plays, and were even invited to perform for the royal family. Wandering Dutch and German troupes, performing in their own languages, were most common in Denmark, and were often invited to perform for the royal family until the 1630s. By that time the Danish aristocrats, through their own travels, had acquired a taste for Italian opera and ballet and were importing troupes for their own entertainment, while the Dutch and German troupes continued to perform regularly for the commoners until shortly after the beginning of the eighteenth century.

The first theatre building was erected in Copenhagen in 1663 by Andreas Wolf. The Dutch Troupe performed there for about three years until the wooden frame building was razed because Wolf was unable to pay his debts. Even after this incident, wandering troupes continued to perform in town squares and in large rooms in various mansions. The format was usually the same: a serious play about a person in the highest circles of government, followed by an improvised farce. In time the popularity of these wandering foreign language troupes waned, and they were almost never seen in Denmark after 1700.

The roots of the national Danish theatre are not found there. What was to become the Danish theatre had its roots in the French acting troupes that the royal family had been supporting at the Court Theatre. The Danish aristocrats were greatly influenced by court life at Versailles. They wanted to follow the new French mode in dress and custom, so they imported French actors to organize a theatre similar to the court theatre in France.

Frederik III brought the first French troupe to the Danish court on 23 August 1669. The troupe, under the direction of Jean Guillemoys de Chesnay Rosidor, received a stipend of five thousand rixdaler a year. The king had charged Rosidor to assemble the best French troupe that could be found anywhere. Rosidor took the challenge to heart, hiring the finest French actors and actresses available. The project was well underway when Frederik III died in February 1670; however, the new king would not provide the promised funds, so the French troupe was dismissed after only six months in Copenhagen.

The Danish court continued to invite touring French companies to perform whenever they were in Denmark, but none were subsidized until Christian V ordered a new troupe of actors in 1682. Apparently the economic situation at court had improved. The troupe, under the leadership of Jean de la Garde (Bouillart), presented the best in French plays. Whatever was popular in Paris was presented for the Danish royalty and their guests.

In 1685, King Christian V's mother, Sofie Amalie,

died. The king's sorrow was so great that he dismissed the French troupe. Six of the actors remained in Denmark, including René Magnon de Montaigu, who eventually laid the foundation for the Danish theatre. Montaigu was born in France in 1661, the son of historian and playwright Jean Magnon. Because of the friendship between Magnon and Molière, it seems likely that Montaigu obtained his theatre training from Molière. After the French troupe was dismissed, Montaigu remained in Copenhagen working at various tasks: directing the royal parties and festivities, arranging for expensive French products for the queen, and working as secretary to statesman Poul Løvenørn. He also married a young French-Danish actress, Marie Magdalene la Croix.

In 1701, the next king, Frederik IV, assembled a third French acting company for the royal court. Montaigu was appointed its leader. The company consisted of seven actors and five actresses; later a technical director, a ballet master, four dancers, and two singers were added to the company. It performed for the aristocracy in the Lille Giethus on Kongens Nytorv and in various large halls. It was also brought to the royal castle, Christianborg, for special performances.

A new opera theatre was completed in 1703. It was the plan that the new building would be available for visiting opera companies, but Montaigu was soon using it for the presentation of French comedies. The actors left the opera house (which was then converted to an army barracks) in 1710, moving into the newly completed theatre in the royal castle.

Montaigu's ability as a theatre administrator is attested to by the fact that the turnover of actors in his troupe was very low. The performers worked well together. They also enjoyed living in Copenhagen. Since they were French, they could associate with the aristocracy; but more than this, they could settle down and have normal, middle-class lives with their families. The king also took good care of them; when they wished to visit France he would provide transportation and servants for them so that they could travel in style. Montaigu made four trips to France in order to gather the latest in popular French plays: Regnard's *The Residuary Legatee*, Dancourt's *The Village Feast*, and, of course, the staple of the French theatre, plays by Molière.

Things went well for the French actors until 1721 when the king's son, Christian, and his bride went to Germany on their honeymoon. There they became so enthralled with German opera that, on their return to Denmark, they convinced the king to dismiss the French actors and engage a German opera company. This was a hard blow to the French actors who had settled down to a routine family life. They petitioned the king for severance pay and money to travel back to France, but were denied both. In order to earn a living, Montaigu decided to open a private theatre. He petitioned the king for permission to build a theatre on Lille Grønnegade (now Ny Adelgade) for the presentation of French comedies. Permission was granted and the theatre was completed in late 1721. *L'Avare* opened the theatre on 19 January 1722.

Unfortunately, the Danish populace would not support the private French theatre. It was closed in February and the actors made their way back to France—all except Montaigu. He had lived most of his life in Copenhagen and decided that he would rather remain there. Not a man to give up, Montaigu decided to try one more private theatre enterprise. He wanted to open another French theatre, but had no actors; and because he had no money to bring new actors to Copenhagen from France, he decided to try to recruit Danish actors. This posed another problem, since Montaigu had lived in Copenhagen for thirty-six years without bothering to learn Danish! He acquired a partner, Etienne Capion, who could speak Danish and who had, incidentally, received royal permission to hold a monopoly on theatre productions in Copenhagen. They petitioned Frederik IV on 1 July 1722 for permission to open the first Danish language theatre. The king approved and gave Montaigu permission to use the theatre building on Lille Grønnegade. So Montaigu began searching for Danish actors.

Montaigu had more serious problems than merely finding and training actors. Even though various theatre productions had been given in Denmark for over one hundred and fifty years, they were always performed in foreign languages. There were no Danish playscripts.

Frederik Rostgaard, chief secretary of the chancellery, and U. A. Holstein, the royal chancellor, were eager to promote the arts. They apparently were responsible for providing a Danish repertoire. The task of translating some of the popular French court comedies, chiefly Molière's, was given to some young justice clerks. Ludvig Holberg, who was known to be "Hans Mikkelsen," the author of *Peder Paars*, was asked to write original comedies for the Danish stage. Holberg had great respect for Molière's comedies, which he knew, most likely, through reading and possibly through seeing them at court in

Copenhagen. His familiarity with Molière, coupled with the fact that Montaigu's entire experience had been the staging of French comedies, certainly affected the form of the plays Holberg was to write. At any rate, Holberg soon began to write scripts whose form was based on French theatre conventions.

THE LITERARY SOURCES OF THE COMEDIES

When Holberg was asked to write for the new Danish theatre, he had just emerged from the *Peder Paars* experience. Even though the work was popular, Holberg felt that it had failed in its purpose. He had succeeded with his colleagues when he satirized Højer, but they were not impressed when he satirized their own weaknesses. Holberg had failed to get his message to those whom he wished would embrace it. He was now searching for a new way to approach his same old theme, and he felt that the theatre would be perfect.

Holberg wrote that a playwright had to accomplish two things: "First, be a philosopher. He must understand the ridiculousness of men. Second, he must have the talent to construct his comedies so they are logical and entertaining. . . . And the comedies must follow the laws of common sense."[4] Holberg also believed that a play must give the central character the opportunity to show off his foolishness. The play should be humorous, festive, and gay, but the writer must use his restraint so as not to fall into the trap of using cheap laughs to delight the gallery.

Most socially concerned playwrights throughout

Western dramatic literature have used tragedy as the
vehicle for examining social issues, but not Holberg.
He was opposed to tragedy; he considered its unnatural
speech, stories about noblemen, and tragic endings pure
affectation. Molière's comedies, especially the character
comedies, best suited Holberg's view of life. Holberg felt
that the attempt to display men's foibles with the intent
of helping them to better themselves epitomized the
ideas of "Nature and Man" that so heavily influenced his
thinking. It is not surprising that Holberg wrote, "Molière, with his rational thinking, has done more to better
the world with his comedies than all of the serious prat-
tlings of all the world's old philosophers."[5] Molière's
comedies greatly influenced the form of Holberg's. The
major elements used by Holberg were the stock family
characters (who in turn had been borrowed by Molière
from the commedia dell'arte), the method of displaying
the central character's foible, a few basic story forms, and
other comic business.

As in Molière's *Tartuffe*, much of the humor of Holberg's plays derives from the way the central character's
foible affects the other members of the household.
Holberg borrowed Molière's basic structure: the introduction of the family group, the introduction of the main
character, the display of the foible, and the main character's recognition of the foible. For example, in *Jean de
France*, Holberg first introduces the family awaiting the
return of their son from France. They worry that the boy
will be affected as so many youths who traveled to France
had become. Then Jean de France is introduced and his
manners are indeed intolerably affected. Jean's foibles are
then ridiculed in several comic ways. Finally, a plan is

devised and carried out to expose Jean's foibles and possibly cure him of them. The construction of *Jean de France* is similar to that of *Tartuffe*: first the character is talked about and then is shown to have the fault in question.

The approach was useful to Holberg in another way. Going to the theatre was not a common practice for most people in Copenhagen during Holberg's time. He found that first clearly developing the story and then showing the absurdity of the central character's quirk was a very useful technique that enabled his public to follow exactly what was going on and to enjoy the humor of the situation.

Even though Holberg had decided that his comedies should ridicule vices that other playwrights had not already depicted, he did borrow from the stories of three Molière comedies. *The Eleventh of June* is derived from *Monsieur de Pourceaugnac*, some of the action of *The Honourable Ambition* and *Don Ranudo* is taken from *Le bourgeois gentilhomme*, and *The Fortunate Shipwreck* has elements of *Les femmes savantes*. Though Holberg borrowed from Molière for these plays, he adapted Molière's plot structure to his own dramatic purpose. Finally, Holberg borrowed comic business from Molière's plays. For example, even though Holberg never wrote a play with a doctor as the central figure, he sometimes ridicules doctors. And, as in Molière, Holberg's doctors often use amusing Latin phrases. In Holberg's *The Maternity Room*, a new mother is talking to her doctor:

MOTHER I've been having the most terrible nightmares. What could be causing them?
DOCTOR There are different kinds of dreams. There are *som-*

nia divina, diabolica, and *naturalia.* Or as Hippocrates claims, only *somnia divina* and *naturalia.* [act III, scene 5]

Now compare Holberg's dialogue with the following from Molière's *Le médecin malgré lui:*

SGANARELLE   Give me your attention please.
GERONTE   I'm doing so.
SGANARELLE   It's caused by the acidity of the humours engendered in the concavity of the diaphragm, it so happens that these vapours—*Ossabandus, nequeys, nequer, potarinum, quipsa milus* and that's precisely what makes your daughter dumb.[6]   [act II]

In both *The Maternity Room* and *Le médecin malgré lui,* patients want to know about their problems. In both plays the doctor answers in Latin, confusing the patient. A major difference, though, is that Holberg's Latin is correct and relevant while Molière's is nonsense and irrelevant.

In one play, *The Busy Man,* Holberg uses the same comic business of Molière's *Le malade imaginaire* throughout the entire play. Even though the central characters of the two plays are totally different, and the situations which motivate the action are different, they seem strangely alike in the incidental comic business. Both Argan, in *Le malade imaginaire,* and Vielgeschrey, in *The Busy Man,* reject their daughters' lovers—Argan for a doctor and Vielgeschrey for an accountant. In both plays the father announces to the daughter that he has selected a husband for her. The elated daughter believes that it is the same man as her secret lover and is happy, until she discovers she has been betrayed; then she is disillusioned and unhappy. In both plays, the fathers choose veritable idiots for the daughters to marry. And both young men address other women, thinking them to be their intended brides. Even though Holberg did borrow comic business from *Le malade imaginaire* and from other plays, he was able to adapt it to his own stories.

The commedia dell'arte also influenced Holberg's comedies. However, his experience with it does not seem to be drawn from its earliest, most traditional form. A study of Holberg's scripts indicates that he was influenced only by the commedia dell'arte which flourished in France in the late seventeenth century. Even though he had apparently witnessed one performance in Italy, his knowledge seems to have been primarily obtained from the reading of commedia dell'arte scripts, specifically those collected by Evaristo Gherardi in 1700. The collection consists of fifty-five scripts that had been produced in Paris between 1682 and 1697. Holberg may also have had access to a collection of Domenico Biancolelli's scripts, which had been performed in the French provinces in the early seventeenth century. Holberg shares three characteristics with commedia dell'arte: the basic commedia story formula, commedia derived character types, and various comic business.

Most of the plays in the Gherardi collection employed a specific story formula: first, the *amorosa*'s father refuses to allow her to marry the *amoroso* because he believes that he has a more advantageous match for her; second, Columbine, the *amorosa*'s servant, invents a series of intrigues which Arlequin, the *amoroso*'s servant, must execute and which invariably involve the disguising of one or both of the servants; and finally, through the use of the intrigues, the *amorosa*'s father is tricked into allowing the marriage of the young lovers. Holberg uses this formula in eight of his plays: *Jean de France, Jacob von Tyboe, The Busy Man, Pernille' s Short Experience as a Lady, Don Ranudo, The Honorable Ambition, The Fortunate Shipwreck,* and *Journey to the Spring*. However, Holberg never uses the formula as the primary storyline of his plays, but instead as a convenient and very effective means of exhibiting and exploiting his own character's foibles. For example, the servant who dons the disguise in *Jean de France* does so in order to allow Jean to exhibit his affectations to their utmost extreme: reversing his clothing and smearing snuff around his mouth because he is duped into believing they are the current French mode.

Holberg also uses character types similar to those in commedia dell'arte but in a modified form. Holberg's Henrich is derived from Arlequin (in fact, Holberg names him Harlequin in *The Invisible Ladies*), Pernille from Columbine (also in *The Invisible Ladies*), Arv from Pierrot, Leander from the *amoroso*, and Leonora from the *amorosa*. However, these characters do not dress in the traditional commedia dell'arte costumes, nor do they assume the traditional commedia personalities.

Finally, Holberg's plays use some of the commedia dell'arte business (as did Molière's). The most striking similarity of business is found in *Journey to the Spring*, which seems to be modeled after the commedia play *The Baths of the Porte Saint-Bernard*. The stage directions for *The Baths of the Porte Saint-Bernard* state: "The back of the stage opens and discloses the Seine above La Porte Saint-Bernard. One sees many covered boats, and bath tents, and a long line of carriages on the banks of the river. Many boatmen make abusive gestures at one another. . . ."[7] The stage directions for the interlude of *Journey to the Spring* state: "The back of the stage is opened where the spring is seen. Around it are many small tents." Both of the stage directions go on to explain a comic pantomime which takes place in front of the background. Thus, Holberg's use of commedia as a source is limited to some story outlines, character relationships, and stage business.

Even though Holberg borrowed abundantly from the form and elements of the plays of Molière and the late seventeenth-century French commedia dell'arte, almost none of his beliefs or themes are derived from them. Instead he used these forms as a skeleton on which to hang his own characters and messages. Even from the first, Holberg had no intention of merely copying Molière's comedies, or any other style of theatre. It was his intention to compete with them. He even contended that *his* plays were far superior for *his* audience. "Several of Molière's comedies are absurd for the average audience member. My Danish comedies are more for the eye than for the ear. For example, *Le misanthrope*, Molière's masterpiece, is just a beautiful and clever conversation which lacks both the festive spirit and situation that compels the audience to laughter."[8] It was Holberg's intention to use these dramatic forms as stepping stones in the creation of his own Danish comedy.

The major influence on the mood and message of Holberg's plays seems to have been English drama and literature. While it is undeniable that Holberg had an extensive knowledge of French drama, that knowledge was chiefly derived through reading. On the other hand, Holberg's knowledge of English life and literature was derived from his happy stay in England from 1706 to 1708: "Since learning is there (in England) held in so great honour, it is no wonder that Englishmen have won the foremost place in both learning and literature. . . . It is believed in this respect that I have adopted something of the character of Englishmen. . . . I pleased them and they pleased me. And, in truth, I seem to be a remarkably faithful copy of them both in manners and in disposition."[9]

Shakespeare is usually the major English influence upon playwrights in other countries, but not so with Holberg. Holberg never mentions Shakespeare. Instead, he was apparently most influenced by the comedies of Ben Jonson and George Farquhar. Holberg singled out Jonson, whose satires "castigate and amuse at the same time, and censure not one, but all faults, not those of one country, but of all mankind."[10] There are almost no similarities in the form or style of Holberg and Jonson; Jonson's real influence is in the delineation of character. Even though Holberg used the French play format, his characters fit Jonson's definition of a "humour":

> As when some one peculiar quality
> Doth so possess a man, that it doth draw
> All his affects, his spirits, and his powers
> In their confluctions, all to run one way.[11]

The study of Holberg's comedies leads one to conclude that even though Holberg was like Molière in form and in the manner of showing off his characters' domination by one foible, he is more like Jonson in ". . . permitting it (these foibles) to assume the force of monomania. Holberg and Jonson, furthermore, had the same general conception of the proper function of a plot. They both believed that almost its sole duty was to exhibit various aspects of the slavery of an individual to a single dominating characteristic."[12] The major difference in the achievement of this goal is that in each play Jonson creates an entirely new setting with different characters, locations, and atmospheres to show his character's manias, while Holberg almost always uses the same characters, locations, and atmosphere, changing only the story line to show his character's foibles.

The plays of Jonson and Farquhar also demonstrated to Holberg that comic characters need not be aristocrats. They showed their audience life outside of London; they took English drama to the farm and to the inn. Holberg followed (reaping much criticism from his learned colleagues) by showing his audience the life of Danish commoners. A Zealand farm is the setting for *Erasmus Montanus*, the recovery chamber of a new mother is the setting for *The Maternity Room*, and Jeppe, in *Jeppe of the Hill*, is thrown onto a dung heap.

It appears that the only manner in which the form of these English plays influenced Holberg is in the closing of a play with a verse pointing out the moral.

Holberg's plays are, though, radically different from the plays of the English Restoration. In epistle 241, Holberg complained that these comedies were full of "difficult and pompous expressions which one does not comprehend at first glance. . . . The English plays are full of such metaphors. I would not dispute the nation its taste on this account, but I remark only that other nations find such grandiloquence loathsome."[13] It is humorous when Holberg refers to his own taste as that of "other nations," but his point is made. He disliked the complicated intrigues and affected language of the Restoration comedies. His distaste is not difficult to understand since the Restoration plays were written for an elite audience, whereas Holberg was writing for a general audience.

While the comedies of Molière, the commedia dell'arte, and the comedies of Jonson and Farquhar exerted the greatest influence upon Holberg's plays, some minor influence is found in the classic Roman comedies. Since many of the commedia devices date back to the Roman comedy, it is difficult to pinpoint any direct influence on style. However, three of Holberg's comedies seem to be based upon Plautus: *The Invisible Ladies* on *Mostellaria*, *Diderich—Terror of Mankind* on *Pseudolus*, and *Jacob von Tyboe* on *Miles Gloriosus*. These three plays are among Holberg's least significant works in terms of popularity and critical comment. In them, he seems to have concentrated more on copying details rather than on adapting borrowed devices to his own plays as he did with the comedies of Molière.

The literary sources of Holberg's comedies are totally independent of any earlier Danish or Norwegian literature. Holberg felt that the average Dane "reads nothing in poetry but congratulatory occasional verse, nothing in theology but funeral orations and sermon books, almost nothing in drama but old stories of Adam and Eve."[14] He hoped that his comedies could help to awaken his fellow countrymen to modern European thoughts. And in writing his comedies, he opened the door to new thoughts and ways of life.

TWO

An Introduction to the Comedies and the Criticism

SINCE MOST OF HOLBERG'S PLAYS are generally unknown outside of Europe, it seems useful to begin an examination of his scripts by acquainting the reader with their general nature and what critics have said about them.

THE COMEDIES

Holberg wrote his first twenty-four comedies in little more than two and one-half years, from the summer of 1722 through the winter of 1724. Three more were written between early 1725 and the closing of the Danish theatres in 1728. Believing that the theatres would not be reopened, Holberg did not write another play for over twenty years. When the theatres were reopened, he wrote his final six comedies between 1750 and 1753.

Although there are slight differences between the first twenty-seven and the final six comedies, the unusual circumstances under which they were written make it impractical to approach the study of Holberg's comedies in a developmental manner. Because of the rapidity with which the plays were written, it is not feasible to trace any maturation process from play to play, as one can when studying the plays of Ibsen, O'Neill, or even Neil Simon. Neither is there any noticeable change in political, religious, or philosophic views from play to play. They seem to have sprung from the mature mind of the playwright almost simultaneously. This consistency from play to play is also evident when comparing the final six comedies with the first twenty-seven. Holberg expresses similar ideas in similar dramatic forms even though more than twenty years had lapsed between their writing. The only minor difference occurs in the plays *Plutus* and *Sganarel's Travels to the Philosophical Land*, where Holberg examines ideas instead of foibles. But even in these plays he uses the same general form as in his other comedies.

Since neither of the traditional categories of chronological or philosophical development is appropriate for the study of Holberg's comedies, another method of classification must be found. While some scholars have categorized the plays for their own purposes, there is no traditional method for classification. The following system is original and provides a useful way to call attention to subtle differences within the scripts. The six general categories into which I have sorted the comedies are (1) comedies of character, (2) comedies of intrigue, (3) comedies for special social occasions, (4) topical comedies, (5) philosophical comedies, and (6) satires of dramatic forms. The plays are grouped according to the dominant element in each script. A play classified as a character comedy or as a comedy for a special occasion does not necessarily exclude the use of intrigue; it does mean that the intrigue, if used, is secondary to other elements of that script. Several characteristics of the comedies are present in all of the categories, such as the repeated use of certain character names and personality types, the use of intrigues, and similar story structures.

Comedies of Character

Sixteen of Holberg's thirty-three comedies are comedies of character, which also tend to be his most popular and critically acclaimed plays. The action of each character comedy is based upon the exploitation, and often correction, of some undesirable personality quirk of the central character. The method of displaying those quirks suggests two subclassifications: family character comedies, in which the main character's foible disrupts an otherwise normal family's happiness, most often keeping young lovers apart; and individual character comedies, in which the individual himself is placed into jeopardy by his foible.

Eight of the character comedies involve the family. These are, with the foibles they ridicule: *The Busy Man* (disorganization), *Jacob von Tyboe* (bravura), *Jean de France* (the pretentious veneer of the French-loving Danes), *The Honourable Ambition* (social climbing), *Don Ranudo* (false pride), *Fortunate Shipwreck* (misjudgment of character and flattery), *The Republic* (political gullibility), and *Erasmus Montanus* (the sophomoric student).

The story of *The Fortunate Shipwreck* will serve to

illustrate the family character comedy. Leonora is in love with the satirical poet, Philemon. But her father, Jeronimus, and stepmother, Magdelone, do not approve of Philemon or his poetry. They are arranging a marriage between Leonora and the hunchbacked writer of flattering verse, Rosiflengius. Leonora, Philemon, and the servants Henrich and Pernille see through Rosiflengius's hypocrisy: he wants to marry Leonora only because her family is wealthy. An intrigue is devised to unmask Rosiflengius's true character to Jeronimus and Magdelone. A whore is sent to Rosiflengius to seek a complimentary verse for her supposed wedding; a drunk and a known swindler seek poems depicting their good characters; and Henrich, dressed as a woman, seeks a poem commemorating a dead dog. Rosiflengius readily sells appropriately flattering poems to each of them. Philemon gathers these verses together for future use.

Later, when Rosiflengius is visiting Jeronimus and Magdelone, Henrich, disguised as a Dutch sailor, enters in a panic. In broken Danish mixed with adulterated Dutch, he informs Jeronimus that his merchant ship has been lost at sea, destroying him financially. Rosiflengius immediately begins making excuses to avoid marrying Leonora. Philemon then enters and is informed of the disaster. He expresses his love for Leonora and promises financial aid to the family until they can re-establish themselves. Jeronimus and Magdelone are grateful and promise Leonora's hand in marriage to Philemon. The wedding arrangements being made, Henrich again laments the loss of the ship, but his wording informs Jeronimus that it is his neighbor's ship which has been destroyed and not his own. Rosiflengius has another quick change of heart and again wants to marry Leonora. His true nature exposed, he is chased out as Jeronimus exclaims, "What a fortunate shipwreck!" But they have not heard the end of Rosiflengius, who vows revenge upon Philemon.

The usual family character play ends with the exposing of the foible and the completion of the intrigue. But the fifth act of *The Fortunate Shipwreck* carries the satire one step further. Rosiflengius gathers his friends and sues Philemon for slander. They testify that Philemon has written slanderous poems against them personally, even though their names were not included in the verses. (These characters, "coincidentally," possess the very foibles of the main characters in Holberg's other character comedies.) After their testimony, Philemon admits to writing the satirical poetry, pointing out that he was satirizing various undesirable human foibles and not individuals. He then produces the flattering poetry Rosiflengius wrote for the whore, drunk, swindler, and dead dog. The judge leaves to consider his verdict, giving the impression that he favors Rosiflengius. After Rosiflengius gloats over Philemon's sure imprisonment, the judge returns and decides in favor of Philemon. He scolds the witnesses and suggests that Philemon should write satirical verses directed against them specifically. Rosiflengius is made to pay the court costs and is forced to wear a dunce hat while he returns home through the main streets of Copenhagen. Philemon and Leonora are overjoyed, and Jeronimus invites the judge to their wedding.

This play is typical of the family comedies because of the gullibility of Jeronimus and Magdelone in believing the flattery of Rosiflengius (whose name literally means "to flatter indiscriminately"). They are so overwhelmed by his compliments that they wish to force their daughter to marry him against her will. This particular script is double-edged in that it ridicules both flattery and the believing of flattery. And, at the end of the play, the foibles of both the flatterer and the duped parents have been exposed. Jeronimus and Magdelone are cured of their foible, while Rosiflengius is punished because of his: it is likely that he will be forced to give up his dishonest occupation. The intrigue of this comedy typifies the family comedies in that its main purpose is the uniting of young lovers through the exposing of the central character's faults. This script also suggests that on some occasions in his career, Holberg wanted to talk to his audience about his role as a satirist. Like most writers of satire, he found it necessary to cover himself.

The eight individual character comedies are similar to the family plays in that they display an undesirable quirk of the main character. But in these comedies, a well-defined family is not presented; instead, the main character himself is ridiculed by his peers, who then devise an intrigue to expose and possibly cure the foible. The foible places into jeopardy the central character rather than someone around him. These plays and the foibles they satirize are *The Political Tinker* (armchair politicians), *Jeppe of the Hill* (inability of the untrained individual to handle authority), *Gert Westphaler* (over-talkativeness), *The Fickle Woman* (indecisiveness), *The Bridegroom's Metamorphosis* (widows who attempt to marry young men), *Without Head or Tail* (fanaticism of both overly liberal and overly conservative beliefs), *The Philosopher in His Own Estimation* (armchair philosophers), and *The Arabian Powder* (gullibility of believing in alchemy).

The *Political Tinker*, one of Holberg's most successful comedies, typifies this group. Through conversations between Antonius, Henrich, and Geske von Bremen, it is established that Herman von Bremen has become so fanatically involved with the discussion of politics that he is neglecting his family and his business. The "political college" of von Bremen and his tradesmen friends is displayed in all of its ridiculousness as the members discuss the then current political issues: Vienna's lack of a navy, the reason why Hamburg (where the play takes place) should be colonized, the need for reformation of marriage laws, and the need to choose the mayor from among the common tradesmen instead of from among the politicians. The next scene indicates that this political college has been getting quite a reputation outside of von Bremen's sphere because two city officials, Abraham and Sanderus, are joking about it. They decide to teach von Bremen a lesson and demonstrate how ridiculous his political beliefs really are. So they set the intrigue in motion by informing von Bremen that he has been chosen mayor due to the ideas he advocated in his political college.

Von Bremen's inability to conduct himself appropriately either politically or socially as mayor is next exploited. Abraham's and Sanderus's wives visit the von Bremen home and are aghast when Geske von Bremen serves syrup in their coffee. Friends of the scheming city officials soon bombard von Bremen with problems which he must solve. He becomes more and more overwhelmed by the tasks he is called upon to perform. When von Bremen has been tormented almost to the breaking point, he is informed that he is not actually the mayor and that his actions should prove to him that such men as himself are incapable of handling political affairs. Von Bremen is convinced that the officials are right and the story ends. The play concludes with a moralizing verse spoken directly to the audience explaining that the uneducated masses should not concern themselves with political affairs. A minor subplot involving the arrangement of a wedding between Antonius and Engelke von Bremen laces the otherwise satirical play with lighter, less relevant romantic material.

In this play, Herman von Bremen himself, and not his family, is ridiculed and placed in jeopardy. His own inability to handle political matters is depicted, as well as his belief that he can handle such matters better than those in office. The foible does affect his family to the extent that he ignores them, but he is not forcing a family member to do something against his will. The love interest between von Bremen's daughter, Engelke, and Antonius plays only a minor part in the story and is in no way affected by von Bremen's quirk.

Comedies of Intrigue

Both examples of character comedies have demonstrated the use of the intrigue to unmask undesirable character traits. In the intrigue, one of Holberg's most frequently used devices, one or more characters disguise themselves and invent a situation that will trick another person into giving them their own way. Six of Holberg's plays utilize the intrigue as a situation comedy device rather than as a device to expose a foible: *Henrich and*

Pernille, The Invisible Ladies, Pernille's Short Experience as a Lady, Diderich—Terror of Mankind, Abracadabra, and *The Peasant Boy in Pawn.* These comedies of intrigue are similar to a situation comedy series on television; they use the same characters, placing them in different sets of circumstances. *Henrich and Pernille* is a good example:

Leander's servant, Henrich, has gone into the city to take care of some of his master's business. In order to amuse himself, he has donned his master's expensive clothes. While in the city, he meets a beautiful lady and they fall instantly in love. When the scene changes, it is revealed that Leonora's maid, Pernille, has also dressed in her lady's expensive clothes. Henrich and Pernille have met, fallen in love, and become betrothed, each believing the other to be of a higher social class. Each counts on the other to forgive the deception because it springs from overzealous love.

When Leander comes to the city, Henrich tells him about his fiancée. By the description of her clothes, Leander believes that Henrich has fallen in love with his own fiancée, Leonora. Leonora also hears the story from her maid and believes that Pernille has stolen away her lover, Leander. So Leonora and Leander meet, have bitter words, and cancel their wedding plans.

Later, Jeronimus, Leonora's father, comes home bewildered because his once future son-in-law has treated him very coldly. Leonora cries that Leander has just married Pernille. Jeronimus confronts Leander to see what could have caused such a marriage and is thoroughly confused when Leander complains that Leonora has just married his own servant, Henrich. Jeronimus figures out what has happened and is able to quickly resolve the problem. Henrich and Pernille learn that they have actually married within their own social class, and Leonora and Leander renew their wedding plans.

The deception, which is the heart of the intrigue, has begun before the action of the play starts. The entire play is based on the situation resulting from the intrigue; because of the intrigue, comic misunderstandings result. The main objective, then, is the unraveling of the misunderstandings, rather than the exposing of some character fault.

Two of the comedies of intrigue vary somewhat from the others. In both *The Peasant Boy in Pawn* and *Abracadabra*, the purpose of the intrigue is to swindle some unsuspecting person out of his money and/or property. In *Abracadabra*, for example, Henrich and Leander attempt to swindle Jeronimus out of his money by making him believe that his house is possessed by evil spirits. The intrigue results when they attempt to prove the house haunted. Even though these plays differ from the other in intent, both the romantic intrigues and defrauding intrigues focus their action upon a plot to misrepresent someone in some way.

Comedies for Special Public Occasions

Holberg wrote some of his plays by request, for special social events. They were usually performed either on the day of the special event or during the season of the event. These five plays include *The Christmas Room, Journey to the Spring, The Mascarade, The Eleventh of June*, and *The Burial of Danish Comedy*.

The Mascarade is typical of the comedies based upon a series of special public occasions. It tells of a young man whose father has arranged his marriage to the daughter of an old friend. But the boy, against his father's will, goes to a masked ball where he falls in love with another girl. Comic problems result, which are resolved when it is discovered that the "other" girl is the daughter of the old friend. An interesting side point of this popular comedy is that the masked balls were held in the Grønnegade Theatre on nights when plays were not presented.

The Burial of Danish Comedy, written for a single event, is so different from the other Holberg comedies that it is often omitted from anthologies of Holberg's complete comedies and from literary evaluations of the comedies. When Montaigu received notice in the spring of 1728 that the theatre was to be closed, he commissioned Holberg to write a special play for the occasion. When Holberg wrote *The Burial of Danish Comedy*, he thought that he would never again see plays performed in Denmark. This play became the funeral service for the Danish theatre and the performances of his own comedies. In it, actors wonder what they'll be doing in the future; one actor claims that he will become a rabbi, and the theatre manager informs the company that he will become a cook. At the conclusion of the play, a eulogy is read. *The Burial of Danish Comedy* was performed once in 1728, and has never been revived in Denmark.

Topical Comedies

Two of Holberg's plays, *Witchcraft* and *The Maternity Room*, are based upon common social attitudes of his time. These plays were written to satirize general practices or beliefs rather than individuals. *Witchcraft* tells the story of a group of excited people who believe witches have come to plague their village. When the superstitious mob comes to destroy the witches, they learn that the coven is merely a group of actors rehearsing a play about witchcraft. *The Maternity Room* is a biting satire on the customs relevant to the visiting of new mothers. The vehicle for Holberg's consideration of this custom is the story of an old man who is married to a young woman. His friends tease him about his marriage so much that he comes to believe that his faithful wife has cuckolded him. But the main purpose of the play is to expose the parasitic selfishness of those who come to visit the new mother: she must provide them with food, drink, and even money for their troubles. Holberg is also eager to demonstrate how much better off new mothers would be if they were left alone and allowed to rest instead of playing hostess to visitor after visitor.

Philosophical Comedies

The two philosophical comedies, *Plutus* and *Sganarel's Travels to the Philosophical Land*, are Holberg's most abstract, dealing with ideas instead of individual foibles. While they are both concerned with some of Holberg's beliefs, neither of them is a deep or searching play. *Plutus* makes the statement, not only through the action, but literally, that wealth should be distributed blindly because most good men are unable to cope with it. *Sganarel's Travels* ridicules philosophers: Sganarel journeys to the Land of Philosophers seeking wisdom, but when he arrives, he finds that the philosophers are merely men who quibble with one another about trivial matters.

Satires of Dramatic Forms

The final two comedies, *Ulysses von Ithacia* and *Melampe*, are vastly different from the other Holberg comedies and from each other. Both of them were written to satirize dramatic forms which Holberg did not like: *Ulysses von Ithacia*, the bombastic German sagas presented in Copenhagen during the earliest years of the eighteenth century; and *Melampe*, high tragedy.

Ulysses ridicules the German sagas' total disregard of the unities of time and place and their other incongruities. Holberg bases his satire on the familiar stories of *The Iliad* and *The Odyssey*, thus enabling his audience to concentrate on his satire rather than on trying to follow an unfamiliar story line. Helena is kidnapped and Ulysses goes off to Troy to retrieve her. As a comic Trojan War continues, scenes change radically. Years pass between them, aging some of the characters while leaving others unaffected. The generals speak in bombastic language while peasants use the vernacular. Anachronisms abound in the script. After years of failure, Ulysses returns home, only to find that his wife has remarried and that he has lost his kingdom; his former subjects remember him only as someone who went off to find some woman who was not really very pretty anyway. Finally, two Jews appear and tear the clothes off his back because he had gone off to Troy without paying the rent for them.

Melampe lampoons a more familiar dramatic form,

high tragedy. In it Holberg clearly shows his contempt for the noble goals of aristocrats, for the "serious" nature of their stories, and for the use of formal verse for dialogue (he wrote the commoners' dialogue in everyday prose and the aristocrats' dialogue in alexandrines). The story depicts a feud between two aristocratic Italian sisters. One sister has stolen the other's lap dog, Melampe. As the fighting becomes more bitter, a cat is taken hostage, an uncle is accused of being a spy, and the sisters' father, who is dead, appears, begging them to stop their fighting. Finally, a brother puts an end to the feud by cutting the dog in half. The father reappears to reconcile the sisters' differences, and the play ends.

Neither *Ulysses von Ithacia* nor *Melampe* is like any of the other plays. In these comedies, Holberg concentrates upon satirizing certain dramatic forms and, rather than using his usual dramatic structure, bases their structures on the forms being lampooned.

HOLBERG'S AUDIENCE

A deeper understanding of the nature of Holberg's comedies is acquired when their audience is understood. Before he began writing the comedies, Holberg had decided to write them for the public, the newspaper-reading public. His goal was to find the readers and win them over. Holberg wanted very much for his plays to be a *popular* success, and they were. The Danish university students loved Holberg's comedies; they enjoyed seeing the new Danish satires about the people around them. Also, since Holberg was liked by the king, Frederik IV, he was able to write without being censored, which was virtually unheard of at the time. Thus, the university students in Copenhagen considered Holberg's comedies a sort of spiritual emancipation.[1] The middle-class workers and farmers also knew and enjoyed Holberg's comedies. The commoners even went so far as to use the names of Holberg's characters as nicknames for one another. They teased each other by calling a braggart a "Jacob von Tyboe," a sophomoric student an "Erasmus Montanus," a lazy drunk a "Jeppe." This tradition was carried to the late nineteenth century when close friends of the verbose Henrik Ibsen called him a "Gert Westphaler." Theatre records show clearly that, from the very first, Holberg's plays were presented to full houses,[2] and that even the peasants in the gallery were attentive while the plays were in progress.[3] The gallery loved the political satire and loudly gave its approval with laughter and applause.

Since original source material from Holberg's period is scarce, little more is known about the acceptance of Holberg's comedies by the residents of Copenhagen. In fact, most of the available comments are found in Holberg's own writings. It is known, though, that the Danish scholars and aristocrats did not like Holberg's comedies. Available reactions will be cited to better facilitate an understanding of what was liked and what was disliked about Holberg's plays.

HOLBERG CRITICISM

There is no formal criticism coeval with the first productions of Holberg's comedies. The first play critiques of the Danish theatre were written and published in 1771, twenty years after Holberg's death, and almost fifty years after the opening of the Grønnegade Theatre. Some fragments of critical commentary relevant to the original productions of the comedies are available. While none of these refer to any individual comedy's performance, they do provide insight into the attitudes toward the comedies during the 1720s.

The first known comment on Holberg's plays was discovered in the diary of a Swedish major general, Gustav Wilhelm Coyet. Coyet, who had actually come to Copenhagen for subversive political reasons, arrived about the time of the opening of the Grønnegade Theatre. He attended some of the performances of Holberg's plays and was impressed enough to buy one of the first published volumes of the plays in 1723. His subversive activities were discovered, and he was incarcerated. While in prison he wrote a journal in which was found this comment: "I must admit, that while most comedies lose much of their comedy in reading, (Holberg's) lose almost none, if any, of theirs. They contain a fine and beneficial satire about various everyday mistakes of common life."[4]

Even though it is known that the contemporary Copenhagen scholars did not like Holberg's comedies, there are no existing copies of any of their criticism. In 1788, the writings of F. Suhms, a Danish scholar, were collected; in them, a letter was discovered in which he had listed the early scholarly objections to Holberg's comedies and had rebutted them. Other than a few of Holberg's epistles, this letter is the only primary source recording the attitudes of those who opposed Holberg's plays during the early eighteenth century. Suhms noted

that there were four major objections to the comedies:
First, Holberg's comedies are crass and common, imperti-
nent, obscene, and absurd. Second, they are written in
Danish, a language in which it is impossible to write anything good. French is the language in which comedies
should be written; when unpleasant characteristics are
spoken of in French, they still sound good enough to hear
about, while in Danish the same characteristics sound
shocking. Third, Holberg makes fun of important and educated people and makes them look foolish. Finally, the
comedies are about commoners. Who wants to see a play
about peasants? Suhms responds that the people object-
ing to Holberg's comedies are merely those who recognize themselves being satirized. He labels Holberg's opponents "true Jean de France's" (the character to whom
the educated and aristocratic seemed most to object). Using the then traditional labels "French" and "Danish"
comedies, meaning "Molière's" and "Holberg's" comedies, Suhms continues: "A comedy is to show the ridiculous side of men so they can recognize their shortcomings and change their lives. In regard to purpose, Danish
comedies are no different than French. Language does not
make a foible any different."[5]

Holberg also refers in his epistles to some of the objections to his plays. In epistle 66, he notes that while
foreign critics have written favorably about his plays,
they sometimes fault him for two "mistakes": the characters are exaggerated, and the comedies do not always
follow the unities of time and place. Holberg answers
that his exaggeration of character is deliberate and necessary. He claims that the only effect dramas without exaggerated characters have on their audience is to put them

to sleep. Pointing out the effectiveness of exaggeration in such characters as Plautus's Miles Gloriosus and Molière's Harpagon (in *L'Avare*), Holberg concludes that "what academic critics censure is the very soul of comedy." Concerning unity, Holberg agrees that it is usually necessary to observe the rules. "But," he continues, "a good writer of comedy must not make himself such a slave of rules that he rejects a capital story or the most fitting subject for a drama."[6] Remarking that many dramas which follow the rules do not even deserve to be called dramas, he chides the academic critics for being overly concerned with rules and not being concerned enough with the end result of the staged play.

In epistle 112, Holberg lodges a complaint against criticism that is still prevalent among artists: scholars and critics attack works merely because they achieve popular success. Epistle 190, however, is the most important of Holberg's epistles regarding his comedies; in it, Holberg assures his readers that his comedies were not written for scholars and critics, but for the middle-class audience. He condemns armchair critics who study the scripts but never go to see them performed. "Only he who has studied the theatre and felt by experience the effect of a comedy from the stage can pass judgment on a play." Academic study can only result in judgments on style, moral content, and adherence to academic rules. "Many a drama which seems to be insignificant when read can be extremely effective on the stage. A drama's importance and validity is therefore not to be measured by the criticism of learned journalists but by the applause of the spectators, and when I say spectators I mean only those who have a natural and undepraved taste."

By "natural and undepraved taste," Holberg was referring to those people who liked his type of play rather than the new French comedies of manners by such playwrights as Destouches. He claimed that people who enjoyed the new French comedies had acquired "an unnatural desire for spectacular dramas." To prove his point, Holberg cited the failure of those newer French comedies in the popular, as opposed to the court, theatre. He demonstrated that the middle-class, Danish audience always found translations of Molière's plays (i.e., plays like his own) popular, while translations of the unnatural French comedies failed to gain support. He lambasted the comedies of manners then popular with the French, and therefore with the Danish aristocracy. "People of the middle class . . . whose taste has not been depraved, find greatest pleasure in those plays which criticize the country's manners and morals. I infer that their taste is the better and the more natural [than the modern French and Danish aristocratic taste]."

Holberg reacted to his critics very much as Suhms did, indeed as most writers do when challenged with "The Rules." The comedies' success in the theatre was much more significant to him than the approval of his learned colleagues. He believed that the middle-class Danish audience for whom he was writing had better and less affected taste than did the French and Danish aristocratic audiences. Although he felt it necessary to answer certain criticisms of his plays, he did so not "to refute . . . but rather to instruct." And as he instructs, he cannot resist mentioning that his comedies had received high foreign praise.

In keeping with the great artistic "tradition" of posthumous recognition, after Holberg's death the scholars and aristocrats began to accept his comedies—so much so, that only seventeen years after his death in 1771, when the first formal criticism of the Danish theatre began to appear, Holberg's comedies were already accepted by scholars and the upper class as the brilliant foundation of the Royal Danish Theatre's repertoire.

Peder Rosenstand-Goiske began reviewing productions at the Royal Danish Theatre in November 1771. These reviews, published in *Den Dramatiske Journal*, are interesting, but unfortunately are more concerned with actors and scenery than with playscripts. His reviews of the performances of Holberg's comedies do not, therefore, provide much insight into the latter eighteenth-century attitude toward the plays. But Rosenstand-Goiske did consider Holberg's plays to be as great as those of Plautus and Molière, and other illuminating opinions can be gleaned from his reviews. From the 20 November 1771 review of *Diderich—Terror of Mankind*: "Holberg creates dialogue which is completely natural, even for his most grotesque characters. I believe a writer should follow nature as Holberg does." From the 20 November 1771 review of the *The Political Tinker*: "Those who hate Holberg's plays say that only undesirable people are interested in undesirable characters on the stage. I say that this comedy will interest anyone who knows the country as well as Holberg. . . . Even though some of the play is unnatural, such as the part where von Bremen counts to twenty, we must not complain because it is so funny. . . . The play is not as funny as when it was first written because the political situation has changed, but it is still very enjoyable." From the 16 December 1771 review of

Plutus: "Holberg is great because he takes his classic sources and makes their subjects so Danish. However, this is one of his worst plays and I do not understand how he could write such an unnatural and worthless play." From the 6 January 1772 review of the *The Honourable Ambition*: "The play has the problem of not developing the foible well enough before the intrigue is set in motion to cure it."

Rosenstand-Goiske did write one review in which he discussed a playscript in depth. It is the 27 December 1771 review of *Jeppe of the Hill*:

> Even though this comedy has some improbabilities, or at the least, some awkwardness in the theatre; even though the unities are not observed (in fact the story is actually over at the end of the third act); even though the subject of the play is barely suitable for a comedy; in spite of all that, we say that it is very enjoyable. And why? Because of its happy-go-lucky nature and the many true Danish comic tirades it contains.
>
> The action and main character, such as they are written, are barely suitable to a good comedy. Since the main character is a peasant, and since the action has so little interest, it is a distasteful comedy. So no matter how well it is written, no matter how ingenious, how nationalistic, or how funny it is, it can be called nothing more than a farce. And, we believe, it would be a much better subject for a comic opera.
>
> So far as we can see, this comedy has these errors. But it is natural in style and contains, here and there, many characteristics which were typical to our nation in the time Holberg wrote.
>
> We especially are entertained by the dialogue between Jeppe and Jakob Skomager. Jeppe's entire character is natu-

ral, with a few small exceptions where the character is too witty. For example, in the fifth scene of the second act, when Jeppe says, "It is unknown whether he left the world by land or water," one can clearly see that Holberg is witty, but not Jeppe.[7]

And there are simply too many improbabilities in one play. We make these comments about this man's work because he is the father of good taste here in our country and should be immortal to everyone who knows him. We do not point out these errors merely to criticize, but because he is a great writer. We wish to warn his followers not to run after this great man's faults.

In other words, because Holberg was a genius, he was able to write an enjoyable play even though he broke innumerable rules. Those playwrights with less ability, trying to emulate Holberg, will be wise not to follow his faults. Rosenstand-Goiske also noted, in far fewer words, specific characteristics in Holberg's comedies which he thought *should* be emulated by new playwrights. From the 7 November 1771, review of the *The Busy Man*:

> The story is superbly structured and has original characters. It is full of true comic situations, logical story, and witty dialogue (which is always true of Holberg's plays). The author has created a very natural play. Even though he is a disciple of Plautus and Molière, he always creates a situation and writes dialogue that is typically Danish. This is such an important trait, all too rare among writers who have followed him. . . . Some people do not like Holberg's comedies because, they say, his characters are too overbearing—he carries things too far. But his comedies bring out the true grotesqueness of the characteristics he is ridiculing.

In conclusion, Rosenstand-Goiske preferred plays which "followed nature," were true to life. He liked the fact that Holberg's characters, while exaggerated, were "natural" in that they resembled real people, he also liked the fact that the Holberg characters so well satirized the Danish people and their own quirks. He lauded Holberg for his wit, except when it was used in the dialogue of characters whom he felt should not be witty. Finally, Rosenstand-Goiske felt that anyone who knew Denmark as well as Holberg did would enjoy the plays, even if he or she considered Holberg's characters undesirable.

The criticism of performances of Holberg's comedies since the eighteenth century has, unfortunately, followed the same general pattern of Rosenstand-Goiske's criticism: the acting and scenery are reviewed rather than the scripts. Only occasionally will a critic comment on the script in passing, as in Edvard Brandes' remark: "It is unfortunate that our audiences do not know the German comedy that Holberg satirized in *Ulysses von Ithacia*, because it would make the play funnier to them."[8] Instead of commenting on the scripts, the critics usually compare actors and discuss approaches to the characters in much the same manner as English critics discuss various Hamlets.

Modern writings on Holberg's comedies assume their greatness, in much the same way that critics assume Shakespeare's plays to be great. Edvard Brandes (*Holberg og Hans Scene*, 1898) rhapsodizes about the comedies in an emotional, rather than a scholarly, manner. Jørgen Stegelmann classifies the plays, but his categories—(1) masterpieces, (2) should absolutely be read, (3) ought to be read, (4) read if you must, and (5) not of much value—are listed without any comment or explanation; he simply divides the scripts according to his evaluation of their merit. Twenty-four of the comedies are classified in the highest three categories.[9] The most important examination of the comedies is provided by Hans Brix, who wrote an excellent introduction for the general reader. He gives the literary background and supplies a brief analysis of each play, following as nearly as possible the order in which they were written. His information and insights establish an invaluable foundation for studying the comedies.[10]

What techniques did Holberg use, what devices did he employ, that have enabled his comedies to succeed more than two hundred and fifty years after their writing? The remaining chapters will examine the various components of Holberg's scripts that make his comedies succeed.

THREE

The Comedies on Stage

THROUGH THE AGES, playwrights have written scripts adapted to the particular physical theatre available to them. The Athenian tragedians wrote for the Theatre of Dionysus. A chariot drawn by horses could easily be driven into the acting arena when Aeschylus's *Oresteia* was performed; later, in the same play cycle, bloody scenes could be revealed through the use of the *ekky-klema*. Shakespeare's scripts call for ghosts to appear, for hiding places, for instant changes of location from place to place and from outside to inside; yet all these demands were easily met in the versatile thrust stage of the Elizabethan theatre. Holberg also wrote for a specific theatre, the Lille Grønnegade Theatre. Our knowledge of the interior and exterior of this theatre is very limited; there is not so much as a sketch or a ground plan of the building. Alfred Jeppesen's research indicates that it was a half-timbered structure about the same height as a standard two-story building, but without the usual separation between the floors. Based on a 1720s deed, it can be estimated that the theatre was about one hundred feet long and forty-five feet wide. Behind the theatre building was a spacious courtyard and a large garden with two small buildings which, in the summer, were used as refreshment stands. The entire courtyard was enclosed by a plank fence with a gate opening on Gothersgade.

The layout of the theatre's interior is also uncertain. It is likely that the stage area occupied half of the available space. Presumably there were also a pair of benches on the floor just under the proscenium for musicians. The audience area, which could probably seat between four and five hundred people, included fourteen orchestra loges (the lower boxes), sixteen balcony loges (the upper boxes), and over these, the gallery benches. The handbills always referred to the upper boxes as the "midmost," because of their relation to the orchestra boxes below and the gallery benches above. Each loge seated at least four people. The Copenhagen theatre also followed the contemporary foreign theatre custom of allowing distinguished patrons to be seated on the stage.[1]

As with the building itself, very little is known about the productions in this theatre; there is no record of the stage or its properties. However, through the study of the playscripts which were performed there, some educated guesses can be made about the theatre's facilities.

SCENERY

Montaigu attempted to operate the Grønnegade Theatre as a business. He apparently received no subsidy from either the royal court or individuals, and his first attempt to produce French comedies in 1721 had resulted in bankruptcy. It is logical to assume that little money was available and that the theatre had only the bare necessities of scenery and stage equipment. When the Grønnegade Theatre was reopened for Danish language productions, it was an attempt by Montaigu to make a living at the job he knew and enjoyed. Since he had no extra capital, it seems likely that whatever theatre resources were in existence when the French language theatre closed were the only facilities available to the new Danish language theatre. Since the *look* of Holberg's plays was most strongly influenced by Molière's comedies, and since it is certain that Montaigu at least counselled Holberg regarding the available facilities and at best showed Holberg the facilities in the theatre for which he would be writing, it is likely that Holberg's comedies reflect these available resources.

The French comedies could all be staged with any one of only three backdrops: an interior, an exterior, or a country scene. It is likely that these three were originally the only backdrops available for staging Holberg's plays. An examination of Holberg's scripts supports the three backdrop theory. Most of Holberg's comedies require only a single setting, either the interior of a house or a street scene, and were performed in front of the same backdrops used for the Molière productions. But as soon as Holberg's plays proved to be successful, and at his insistence, a new backdrop was painted for a Danish middle-class interior. A new backdrop for a Copenhagen street scene was probably painted at a later time. The "Danish" backdrops were then used for the Holberg plays and the "French" for the Molière plays. The grove backdrop was used for all necessary country locations in both the Danish and French plays.[2]

Even though Holberg's plays generally were adapted to these settings, a few of the plays posed special problems. For example, the original version of *The Political Tinker* required two different interior settings: the home of Herman von Bremen and an inn. Before being produced, the "political college" scene at the inn was rewritten to take place in von Bremen's home so that only one interior setting was needed. Similarly, the location of the meeting of Jean de France and Madame La Flèche was changed so that only one exterior setting would be needed in *Jean de France*. Holberg evidently rewrote these scripts so they could be staged in only one setting each—strong evidence, indeed the strongest available evidence, that little scenery was on hand in the Grønnegade Theatre.

Another of the earliest Holberg comedies, *Jeppe of the Hill*, calls for the interior of a rich man's mansion. Since no such setting was available, the scene was played before the grove backdrop, with the result that playing the mansion scene in front of the grove backdrop in productions of *Jeppe of the Hill* became a tradition in the Danish theatre lasting until 1903.[3]

Some of Holberg's playscripts do call for certain scenes to be played in the street and others to be played inside. This requirement posed no real problem in plays like *The Maternity Room*: the first act was played before the street backdrop; then, during the break before the second act, the backdrop was changed. But not all of the scripts which call for both interior and exterior settings were so easily changed. A few of them demand exterior and interior action in the same scene without a break. Act IV of *The Fortunate Shipwreck* poses such a problem: most of the act takes place inside the house, but suddenly the characters move outside to the street. Since there is no break in action, it was undesirable to stop the play to change the backdrops. Tradition indicates that this problem was solved by using the interior backdrop throughout. When the characters were to leave the house, they moved down-stage to the edge of the stage for the street scenes. Alfred Jeppesen hypothesizes that a curtain could be drawn at mid-stage to cover the backdrop on such occasions.[4]

The Fortunate Shipwreck is scenically the most demanding Holberg comedy. Act I takes place inside, acts II and III take place on the streets of Copenhagen, act IV takes place both inside and outside, and act V calls for another interior—a courtroom. The final act was apparently staged in the usual interior setting; a judge's bench was moved in and any conflicting furnishings removed. The play was never performed in the Grønnegade Theatre, possibly because of the complicated scene changes, even though it was written during the early years of the theatre's existence. Its production twenty years later at the Royal Danish Theatre, with its better facilities, was first staged in this manner.

One other Holberg script poses a problem with scenery: *Journey to the Spring* calls for the scene to open showing a spring surrounded by many tents. The demand for the "scene to open" supports Jeppesen's hypothesis of the mid-stage curtain. But it is unknown how the required scene was shown in the Grønnegade Theatre, since the theatre certainly did not have the funds available to paint a special backdrop for one play. Probably the scene was improvised or suggested in some way.

Records are available from the Royal Danish Theatre from 1746 when theatres were allowed to reopen in Denmark after being closed for almost twenty years, so it is known how the scenery there looked for Holberg productions. The traditional use of three Holberg backgrounds was retained—further strong evidence supporting the idea that only three scenes were used for Holberg plays in the Grønnegade Theatre. In the Royal Danish Theatre, three wings were added to each side of the stage. The "Holberg Room" and "Holberg Street" backdrops were used for all of his plays until the 1840s, almost one hundred years. Then, Troels Lund painted a new Holberg interior which came to be known as the "Green Room." Even though the Royal Danish Theatre was building box sets for other plays at that time, in the new Holberg set Lund followed the tradition of three wings and a backdrop. He did add two practical doors, though: one between the first and second wings on stage right, and one between the second and third wings on stage left. This set was used until the 1870s.

During the 1870s a new street scene and a box set with practical windows and doors were built. This scenery was used until 1899 when William Bloch totally revamped the production of Holberg's comedies at the Royal Danish Theatre by designing individual, naturalistic settings for each new Holberg production. Between 1899 and 1905 Bloch designed naturalistic settings for eight Holberg comedies, including *Erasmus Montanus*, *Witchcraft*, and *The Maternity Room*. The tradition of playing the mansion scene from *Jeppe of the Hill* in front of the grove backdrop came to an end when Bloch designed his *Jeppe* sets in 1903. Since this time, a new set has been built for each new production of a Holberg comedy.

Thus, Holberg's scripts make a minimal demand upon stage scenery. Most of them can be performed in one setting. Even plays calling for both interior and exterior settings, such as *Gert Westphaler*, were traditionally staged in one setting, even when more money was available for scenery at the Royal Danish Theatre. As the customs of theatre scenery changed, new settings were provided for Holberg's plays, but they did not seem to affect the success of the comedies one way or the other.

Since it is apparent that the lighting in the Grønnegade Theatre was, at its best, inadequate, and since Montaigu's training was with French theatre conventions, the actors in the Danish comedies probably moved similarly to the way it is believed the French actors of the time moved—that is, they remained downstage in front of the backdrops delivering their lines in a very presentational manner. When several characters were on stage, they stood in a semi-circle, moving only when it was required by the script. So the meager lighting and limited visual aspects of early Holberg acting further support the backdrop theory by not making any additional requirements for scenery.

COSTUMES

The limited budget of the Grønnegade Theatre also affected the costuming of Holberg's comedies. It is be-

lieved that some costumes from the original French theatre were still available, and since the clothing of the
Danish upper middle class was generally based upon the
French styles, some of the costumes could be used in
Holberg's plays. However, Holberg did not want all of the
actors in his plays to be attired in the French mode;
French costumes were inappropriate for most of the Danish characters in his plays. Therefore, Holberg's plays
were for the most part costumed with everyday Danish
apparel. This added to the Danish look of the productions
by enabling the actors to resemble the people they were
portraying.[5]

The limited amount of stage movement and the lack
of special costumes support the idea that the visual aspects of the plays contributed only negligibly to their success. As the theatre styles changed, the acting became
more realistic and less presentational. Costumes, too, became more important as money became available for special costumes to be built for each production.

SPECIAL STAGE MACHINERY

Just as Holberg's scripts make little demand on stage
settings, they make little demand on special stage ma-
chinery or effects. In fact, only two special requirements
are made in the plays. In *Without Head or Tail*, a stage
direction in act II, scene 2 states: "Old Eric comes up out
of the ground dressed in black and wearing a horn on his
forehead." Later, Marthe tells Leander about the secret
hole. She ends her speech:

MARTHE . . . I'll stand behind the hole so I can rip the mask off
of her when she rises up.
(*Marthe gives the sign by stamping on the ground. Gunnild
rises up out of the hole.*) [act IV, scene 10]

From the above directions and dialogue, it is apparent
that a trapdoor was needed in the stage. However, it is not
known whether one was previously available, or whether
one was built specifically for this play. Since only absolutely necessary furnishings could be afforded, the building of a special set piece for this effect, in place of a trapdoor, seems out of the question. In any case, a trapdoor of
some kind is essential for the production of *Without
Head or Tail* because action is based upon it throughout
the play. The play also requires a method for lowering an
actor to the stage from above; in scene 3, several gods
enter, including Jupiter and Apollo, who "come down out
of the air." Even though it is not known how much fly
space was available above the stage at the Grønnegade
Theatre, it is clear that no conventional rigging or flying
equipment was available. Nevertheless, it would easily
be possible to lower an actor to the stage with some sort
of temporary pulley system to satisfy the demands in
Without Head or Tail.

This lack of equipment, however, would make it extremely difficult to hoist an actor up from the stage to the
fly space. That difficulty may explain why no Holberg
script required ascension until *Plutus*, which was written
in 1751 after the new Royal Danish Theatre was built.
Here, in act I, scenes 4 and 5, are Holberg's only stage
directions requiring rigging or flying equipment: "Mercurius descends" and "Mercurius is hoisted up again." So,

Holberg's scripts call for a minimum of special stage equipment. Only a trapdoor and a method for lowering an actor to the stage from above were needed in the Grønnegade Theatre. Later, in the Royal Danish Theatre on Kongens Nytorv, a method for raising an actor back up off the stage was necessary.

It is not known whether it was Holberg's inclination, or the fact that he could not talk Montaigu into providing more scenery, or both, that brought about this lack of dependence upon visual aspects of the theatre. But Holberg did not exploit the visual possibilities of a well-equipped stage.

FOUR

Holberg's Characters

FROM THE FIRST PRODUCTIONS of Holberg's comedies in the Grønnegade Theatre, until the present day, the single most commented-upon aspect of his plays is the "Danishness" of the characters. Early eighteenth-century Danish scholars complained that they had no desire to watch plays about lower- and middle-class Danes. On the other hand, the university students and middle-class audience were most enthusiastic in their praise of Holberg for creating such characters. Holberg was also proud of his characters. After stating in epistle 506 that "it has been most difficult for me to invent characters not previously delineated by others," he boasts about the success of the characterization in such plays as *The Political Tinker*, *Without Head or Tail*, and *Jeppe of the Hill*.[1]

An analysis of the characterization in the Holberg comedies indicates that this "Danish" quality is merely an illusion. Holberg adopted universal character types and made them local in appearance. The praise for his "Danish" characters is understandable, though. Most people do not consciously know about universal character types; they know about the people next door. When they see a trait that they recognize, they exclaim, "How like life!"—or, in the case of Holberg's comedies, "How Danish!" A close look at the characters will demonstrate how this illusion is created. Even though all of the characters in the plays must be considered in such an analysis, the general references (including Holberg's own) made about the "Danish characters" refer to the central characters of the character comedies. Therefore, these personae will be examined first.

In the character comedies, Holberg concentrates upon the satirization of particular character traits. But none of these—disorganization, bravura, social climbing, false pride, gullibility—are unique to eighteenth-century Denmark. Such traits have probably existed in all societies and in all ages. Even the foibles in such plays as *Jean de France*, where Holberg specifically satirizes Danes who reject their own culture for that of the French, have similar applications in other cultures. For example, a young woman who was happily active in the university theatre near her home in Ohio recently went to visit New York City just as Hans Frandsen (Jean de France) went to visit Paris. After a short stay in New York, she returned, only to find fault with every aspect of her university theatre because, she said, "It's so provincial."

So the illusory "Danish" quality of the characters does not derive from the fundamental personality traits depicted in the Holberg plays. Its source, however, can be identified when comparing Holberg's plays to those plays which were performed in Copenhagen before the exis-

tence of the Danish language theatre. There was no formal Danish language theatre in Copenhagen before the
opening of the Lille Grønnegade Theatre. Before that
time the Danish audience witnessed bombastic German
sagas about foreign royalty, similar Dutch plays, and
French plays about the upper classes. The social situations and settings of these plays were always foreign to
the middle-class Danes. Furthermore, the plays were always performed in the language of the various acting
troupes instead of in Danish.

On the other hand, Holberg's comedies brought to
the stage characters who had Danish names. The plays
were usually set in Copenhagen and referred to familiar
streets and buildings, such as the Round Tower. But most
of all, the characters were common people straight from
the streets of Copenhagen who spoke the common language, everyday Danish. At this time, scholars and aristocrats felt that Danish was far too vulgar and inferior
a language in which to write. It is significant that Holberg
decided not only to write in Danish, but in everyday
prose rather than verse, a practice that spurned the traditions of most contemporary drama.

The actors also looked, as well as sounded, like everyday Danes. At Holberg's insistence they wore Danish
clothing appropriate for the characters they were playing.
Other aspects of Holberg's characters are unique to early
eighteenth-century Copenhagen. For example, students
and pedants in the comedies have changed their names to
the Latin equivalents. This custom, common throughout
much of Europe during the Renaissance, was still being
practiced in Denmark. Holberg's characters also observe

Danish holidays and customs, as is shown most clearly in such plays as *The Eleventh of June, The Maternity Room,* and *The Christmas Room.* They are preoccupied with politics and activities which preoccupied the Copenhageners of the time. Had Holberg not specified that *The Political Tinker* takes place in Hamburg, the play would seem to take place in Copenhagen because of the settings and the language, and most of all, because the political situations discussed were those being discussed in Copenhagen at the time Holberg wrote the play.

So Holberg's characters are not so uniquely Danish; they can be more correctly described as universal characters identified as Danish. Holberg was so successful in this depiction of the Danish environs that the nineteenth century Danish playwright Oehlenschläger noted: "If Copenhagen were to be utterly destroyed, and in a subsequent generation only Holberg's comedies were to be unearthed, the Copenhagen of the early eighteenth century could be reconstructed from them alone as completely as Pompeii and Herculaneum have been." To this, Oscar Campbell adds, "Not only the great city [could be reconstructed], but also the typical village and farm of Zealand at the same time."[2] But the "Danish" quality of the Holberg characters exists on the superficial level, not on the level of personality. Holberg's plays were written to be performed for the Copenhagen middle class, so he wrote about the Copenhagen middle class. And, since most Western middle classes are similar, the characters are much like people in any Western middle class. If the characters' names, the locations, and the language were changed, the plays would *seem* to depict another society because of the many common characteristics of the Western middle classes.

HOLBERG'S CHARACTERS AND THE COMMEDIA DELL'ARTE

The fact of the matter is that most of Holberg's characters had their origins, not in Danish literature or drama, but in the commedia dell'arte. Indeed, twenty of the thirty-three Holberg comedies use the basic commedia dell'arte personae. As outlined above, Holberg makes these characters seem Danish by transforming the basic family unit of the late seventeenth century commedia dell'arte into a middle-class Copenhagen family with Danish names, speech, and clothing. Generally, the characters are related to those in the commedia dell'arte as follows: the *amoroso* (male love interest) is Leander; the *amorosa* (the ingenue) is Leonora; the manservant, Arlequin, becomes Henrich; the lady's maid, Columbine, becomes Pernille; the rogues, Scapino and Pulcinello, become Oldfux; and the strict, overbearing father, Pantalone, becomes Jeronimus. Holberg's character types are not quite so standardized as those in the commedia dell'arte. Like the Italians, Holberg retains names, relationships, and family structure from play to play, but he allows greater changes in the characters' personalities. For example, as in the commedia dell'arte, the responsibility for the action of the plays rests on the servants, Henrich and Pernille. They are clever in developing intrigues to unite the young lovers and to expose the foibles of the central characters. But the personalities of these characters are not as constant from one play to another as the commedia dell'arte personalities usually are.

Consider the following different personalities bestowed upon Henrich in various comedies. In *Abracadabra* he and his master Leander are rowdy and reckless, like the character of Charles Surface in Sheridan's *The School For Scandal*. Leander is supposed to be managing the money of his guardian, Jeronimus, who is away traveling. Instead, he and Henrich have squandered the funds on riotous living. When they learn that Jeronimus is returning, they realize that they will have to pay for their frivolity. So Henrich comes up with a scheme: they will make Jeronimus believe that his house is haunted and that they had to spend all of his money to acquire a new one. Henrich takes the lead in carrying out the intrigue, which reflects his haughty, bold personality. In *The Mascarade*, Henrich is quite different. Here he is a funloving, witty person who would never harm anyone, let alone help squander money and attempt to cover up the evidence by instigating a scheme like that in *Abracadabra*. He spends his evenings with his master at masked balls, and his days sleeping. When Leander goes to the dances against his father's orders, Henrich persuades the lookout to let them sneak out of the house. Upon arriving at the ball, Henrich does not wait out in the cold; he puts on a mask, goes in, and enjoys the dance. In some of the comedies, such as *The Fortunate Shipwreck*, Henrich is very responsible. And in others, like *The Arabian Powder*, all he does is run errands for his master.

So even though Holberg adapted the stock character types to his own locale and stories, most of his characters have their origin in the commedia dell'arte. Through the use of these stock characters, Holberg enjoyed the convenience of similar relationships from play to play as well as the convenience of established personae with which to tell his stories. This technique is certainly one of the main factors that allowed him to write so many plays in such a short time. Like most writers who have followed the lead of Menander, Holberg did not confine himself rigidly to the traditional personalities. While character relationships may remain similar from play to play, the characters' personalities change somewhat to adapt to their particular situation and story. Yet none of these changes can be said to render the characters Danish in any fundamental way. Holberg's variations are as universal as the commedia models they sprang from.

HOLBERG'S DELINEATION OF CHARACTER

Aristotle suggested that "character" is defined by the choices a person makes; that is, the character of a person is revealed to the audience through the decisions he or she makes. This, however, is only superficially the case with Holberg's personae. They are seldom called upon to make character-revealing decisions, and their characters are manifested only in terms of the choices related to their foible or by their relationship to someone else's foible. Rather than dramatizing character development, Holberg establishes his characters' personalities and their interrelationships by straightforward exposition before the action of the play begins. For example, the most clearly depicted personalities in the comedies are those of the central characters in the character comedies. They all have individual quirks at the time the play begins. All Holberg must do is communicate to the audience, either by monologue or through other characters' discussion of the foible, what the foible is; then the action gets underway to demonstrate the ridiculous extremes of the foible. In the comedies not based upon character foibles, characters are depicted in relation to the central situation or intrigue. In these plays little is done to depict the personalities of the characters; they are more or less "straight." What matters is not who they are, but how they fit into the situation. At any rate, "character" in Holberg's plays is a given entity that is described for, and must be accepted by, the audience as the basis for the action. The plays never show the growth, evolution, or discovery of character except in the most perfunctory sense (for example, when Jeronimus and Magdelone learn that Rosiflengius is a hypocrite in *The Fortunate Shipwreck*). Character is, for Holberg, either the subject for satire or the pretext for situation comedy.

Even though the stories and locales of the character comedies differ greatly in order to ridicule the particular foible, Holberg uses a definite and consistent pattern whereby those foibles are displayed. He first reveals the key personality trait of the central character to the audience by having other characters in the play describe and/or complain about it. Next the central character demonstrates that personality trait through his actions. The ridiculousness of the foible is displayed by carrying it to extremes. Finally, an intrigue is set in motion to expose and sometimes cure the offending individual by taking the foible to preposterous proportions.

For example, in *Jean de France* the character trait is introduced to the audience by Frands and Jeronimus, who are arguing the pros and cons of Frands' having allowed his twenty-year-old son, Hans, to go to Paris. Jeronimus, who has promised his daughter, Elsebet, to Hans, is worried about the youth because of certain letters they have received from him; it appears Hans Frandsen has changed his name to the French equivalent, Jean de France, and now refers to Elsebet as Isabelle and Jeronimus as Jerome. Jeronimus believes that Danish boys should remain Danish and not get caught up in foreign modes. Frands comforts him by explaining that the youth is just showing off the new language he is learning. Frands believes that upon arriving back home in Copenhagen, Hans will again be "Hans" and not "Jean." Just then Frands' servant, Arv, enters to tell them that Hans has just returned from France. But, Arv complains, the boy is almost impossible to understand:

ARV As soon as he entered the door he asked, "Where is mon pear?" I was surprised at such a question. Where the hell can I find a ripe pear in the month of May? I answered, "There aren't any in this country this time of year." Hans was very bewildered by my answer and looked as though he had never seen a Danish orchard. Then he asked about his "tray share mare." I answered that he could find a mare either at Ulfeld's Place or at the Halland Pond, because that's where horses are kept. He thanked me by calling me a dog's name, "Garsong," and other names I won't even mention. [act I, scene 2]

The audience now knows what type of a person to expect: a young man putting on French airs. When Hans

enters, the audience can immediately see his extreme
"Frenchness" by his exaggerated French apparel. Neither
Frands nor Jeronimus can believe his eyes. Nor can they
believe their ears when Hans (Jean) speaks an incredible
mixture of pidgin French and Danish:

JEAN　La la la la la la. I can't quite remember the *bougre de
pagrad* that *Monsieur Blondis* recently taught me. Excuse
me, it's a *grand malleur. Mais voilá mon père et mon
père*-in-law; *bon matin, Messieurs! comment vive ma
chère Isabelle?*

JERONIMUS　Listen to me, Hans Frandsen! I was born on
Christian-Bernikov Street, as was my father. There has
never been an "Isabelle" or "Rover" in our house. My
name is Jeronimus Christophersen and my daughter's
Elsebet, as God is my witness.

JEAN　It's all the same, *mon cher papa*-in-law. Elsebet is *Isabelle* or *Belle. Belle* does have more feeling.

JERONIMUS　Anyone who calls my daughter "Bell" will have
me to contend with! That's a dog's name! If you can't call
us by our Christian names you'll have to find new in-laws.
I'm an old-fashioned, honorable citizen and I don't like all
of these new fads. You'd better listen to me instead of your
highfalutin *parle.*

JEAN　*Pardonnez-moi, mon cher papa*-in-law, one never says,
"new fads," *c'est ne pas bon Parisian, c'est Bas-breton,
pardi.* La la la la. That's the latest *minuet, composé par le
Sieur Blondis. Pardi,* that is an *habile homme, le plus
grand Dantze-maitre en Europe.* Isn't it *"Dantze-maitre"*
in Danish, too? I completely lost my Danish in Paris.

[act I, scene 3]

Hans, now Jean, has displayed the foible himself
both in his attire and in his speech. And this is all the

audience ever learns about him. He is seen exclusively in terms of his foible. After Jean exits, Jeronimus gives Frands just fourteen days to bring Hans to his senses or he will call off the marriage to Elsebet.

Frands goes home to tell his wife, Magdelone, about Hans/Jean. He complains: "I see that he learned to dance a "Fiol de Spain," to sing a lot of love poems, and to destroy his own language. I don't think he can speak either Danish or French!" [act I, scene 5]. But when the boy enters, his mother sides with him. She is delighted by his new mannerisms, believing them to be the mode in Paris. Jean again displays his foible by teaching his mother the new French dance he has been practicing. And since Magdelone believes that he is doing the dance correctly, she allows herself to become a spectacle by dancing absurdly with the boy in the street.

The second act depicts Elsebet, overwrought, fearing her father will force her to marry the ridiculous Jean de France when she is in love with Antonius. So her servants, Marthe and Espen, agree to help her find a way out of the predicament.

In the third act the antics of Jean de France are carried even further. He and his servant, Per, now Pierre, are speaking. Holberg demonstrates that neither of them can, in fact, speak any more French than what they have already displayed, but they belittle the Danish language and attempt to practice their French. Espen starts the intrigue when he appears searching for a Dane by the name of Jean de France. Jean answers:

JEAN   *Je m'appelle Jean de France à votre très humble service.*
PIERRE   I'll translate his answer to Danish. "My name is Hans

Frandsen, at your service." You'll excuse me for having to explain my master's words. He can still understand Danish, but he has difficulty expressing himself. He has just returned from living fifteen weeks in Paris, where he didn't hear one Danish word spoken.

ESPEN   Wow! Fifteen weeks! You certainly have my respect. I've been in the service of the French Lady, Madame la Flèche for only two days and already when I speak Danish I find a French word or two in my mouth. [act III, scene 3]

Espen then goes on to explain that his lady, Madame la Flèche (actually Marthe in disguise), has come to Copenhagen just to meet Jean. Off Jean goes to meet her. The act ends with Jeronimus and Frands again commiserating.

The fourth act depicts the execution of the intrigue. Marthe, disguised as Madame la Flèche, plans to explain all of the new Parisian modes to Jean. After all, she left Paris only twelve days ago by ship, while Jean left four weeks ago by land. She tells the audience, "You know how fast the styles change in Paris." Of course, she and Espen will invent the "new modes." First, Madame la Flèche convinces Jean that the latest in jewelry is a medallion made by nailing an old copper coin to a piece of wood. Jean makes one and hangs it around his neck immediately. When people ridicule him, he laughs at them and tells them how sorry they'll be when the fashion reaches Copenhagen and they all clamor to adopt it. Next, Madame la Flèche expresses her disgust at Jean for being engaged to a Danish girl. Jean grovels and vows to break off his engagement to Elsebet. The real reason for the intrigue has now been fulfilled; Elsebet is free to marry Antonius. But the intrigue continues in order to further ridicule Jean's foible.

Espen enters, as Madame la Flèche's servant; she whispers something in his ear and exits. Espen laughs at what she whispered.

JEAN　*Monsieur le valet de chambre, Monsieur d'Espang!* Why did your lady treat me with such contempt? What did she whisper to you?

ESPEN　If I'd only known earlier, I could have prepared you! But it should be easy to correct. Madame la Flèche said that even though she has great respect for your character, she despises the way you are dressed.

JEAN　Have the styles changed since I left Paris? I toured for a month before returning to Copenhagen.

ESPEN　Yes, Monsieur, you've discovered the problem. Madame la Flèche says that no Parisian cavalier has buttoned his coat like that in weeks! Coats are buttoned in the back now. It may seem a little uncomfortable, but you get used to it. All of the gentlemen have their servants button their coats in the back for them.

JEAN　*Ah malheureux que je suis!*

ESPEN　It's easy to change. I'll help you.

JEAN　*Vous me faîtes un grand plaisir, pardi.*

ESPEN　(*Buttons Jean's coat up his back.*) Now don't you look different!

JEAN　Are there any other changes I should make?

ESPEN　Yes. Fortunately they're all easy to make.

[act IV, scene 4]

Espen goes on to get Jean to smear snuff all around his mouth and to hang his jabot down his back. After Jean has dressed himself in this ridiculous manner and has smeared tobacco around his mouth, he exclaims, "They can invent more gallant styles in Paris in one week than the rest of the world can in a year!"

After Espen exits, Jean converts his servant's clothing to the new styles. But then Jeronimus enters. Jean is insulted when Jeronimus ridicules the way he is attired, so he attempts to instruct Jeronimus in the new styles. When Jeronimus refuses to listen to him, Jean and Pierre assault him, trying to force the new styles on him. Jeronimus calls him a madman and breaks the engagement to Elsebet. Antonius enters, sees Jean and Pierre assaulting the old man, and chases them off. Antonius introduces himself to Jeronimus and declares his love for Elsebet. When Elsebet enters and confirms her love for him, their marriage is arranged.

But the play is not quite over. The ridiculousness of Jean's foible is taken to an even greater extreme. Jean receives a letter explaining that Madame la Flèche could no longer tolerate being in Copenhagen. She has left for Paris and bids Jean to follow and meet her there. Jean decides to go, but first he is stopped by a man who wants to collect one hundred rixdaler that he won from Jean. Jean explains that he has no money, but will be able to send it when he reaches his lady in Paris. Refusing to be put off, the man takes Jean's coat, watch, vest, hat, and wig in payment. Humiliated and penniless, Jean leaves for France. The play ends when a letter is delivered to his father, Frands:

FRANDS (*Reading the letter.*) Madame la Flèche, a respected French lady, has found me too good for Denmark and has invited me to live with her in Paris. Since I am accustomed to the foreign manners and gallantry, and cannot therefore tolerate backward people, such as those in my family, I have decided to join her. I will never return to

Copenhagen. If you write me, address the letter *à la Madame la Flèche, Dame très célèbre et très renommée dans la France.* The letter must be written in French. I have decided that within a few short months I will no longer understand one word of Danish. The letter must be addressed: *À Monsieur Monsieur Jean de France, gentilhomme et grand favorit de la Madame la Flèche, Courtisane tres renommée, dans la Cour de France.* If I am not addressed properly I will return the letter unopened. *Je suis le Votre. Jean de France, gentilhomme Parisien.*

[act V, scene 6]

So Jean leaves Copenhagen without money, bound for a country in which there is no one to take him in, and dressed in a manner that will make him the laughing-stock of Paris. He will either have a rude awakening or fall further and further into the hole he has dug for himself.

Jean de France is the prototype of Holberg's method of depicting character in the five-act character comedies. Even though the stories of these comedies vastly differ, they follow a similar pattern in order to show off best the foible of the central character. As was demonstrated, the foible is first described by the characters whom it affects. Then the central character is introduced and, through his actions, displays his foible. After the trait is demonstrated, its effects on other characters are detailed. In this case, Elsebet does not want to marry a pseudo-French fop, especially since she is in love with Antonius. An intrigue is devised whereby she can be saved from this fate; naturally, the intrigue also demonstrates the ridiculousness of the foible in question. When the purpose of the intrigue is fulfilled, the play can end. If the foible is exposed or cured at the same time that the purpose of the intrigue is fulfilled, the play ends immediately. But in any case, as with *Jean de France,* the play ends only when it has reduced to absurdity the foible of the offender. This play is unique in that Jean never comes face-to-face with his foible. Holberg's other central characters do confront their foibles, resulting in comic business and often in the curing of the foibles. The major portion of the action in the character comedies serves to depict the ridiculousness of the foible. But the individual's characterization is never expanded; it remains the same from start to finish.

The one- and three-act character comedies merely depict a quirk and tell a story in a shorter amount of time. Therefore, the proportion of the script telling the story increases, since the story must be told no matter how much time is allotted for the run of the performance. In these shorter comedies, less time is spent exploiting the quirks of the central characters. The characters are still dominated by their specific traits, but less fun is had at their expense.

The Busy Man is an excellent example of the shorter comedies. To save time, Holberg, like Menander before him, uses a monologue to describe the quirk:

PERNILLE   There have been innumerable comedies written in the world, but not one about a busy man! If there is anyone out there who would like to write one, I can give you plenty of material about my master! You might say that such a character is rare and that no one ever thinks of them, but there are many busy men right here in this country. There are some men who carry on, making enough noise that strangers believe they're insane, even though they are actually doing nothing. Other men might appear to be idle even though they have ten things happening in their heads. I remember one time, a few years ago when I was employed by a country judge. I was traveling with his wife and we had lunch with a woman who wanted very much to impress us. But she overdid everything! First she was in the living room, then the cellar, then she'd be by the cupboard, and then run to the table. She'd yell at her maid and then at her boy. We told her ten times that she shouldn't go through any trouble for our sakes; that we'd be happy with a small sandwich. She wiped the sweat off her face and asked us to be patient for half an hour. My lady swore to me that if she'd known that the woman was so busy she would have eaten at an inn. Finally the table was set. For all her trouble I expected to be served at least a link of sausage. But all of her noise and bother had only created a pot of lumpy oatmeal and eight hard-boiled eggs! But that, at least, was something. If my lord, Hr. Vielgeschrey, with all of his noise, could even come up with an egg it would be more incredible than that old woman. If his business served only to drive away the cold it would be something. That's the way old people keep warm—they run downstairs and then upstairs, and then into the kitchen and soon they don't need any more heat! But my lord works on nothing! I do the least amount of work of any servant in the house, but I'm the only one he compliments. I just act busy. When people ask him how many servants he has, he answers, "Just one. Pernille is my chambermaid, my cook, my cleaning lady, my secretary, my housekeeper, and my wife." Of course that last is a lie; not that I'm any more chaste than anyone else, but he doesn't have time to go to bed with anyone. Besides,

I'm never more beautiful to him than when I have a pen behind my ear, as though I'm doing his bookwork.

[act I, scene 1]

After his foible is described, Vielgeschrey enters with four scribes attending him. He attempts to keep them all working, but in doing so, he cannot remember each of their duties. He becomes confused and actually keeps the scribes from their work. Next he sits down to write an important letter, but after barely beginning it, he jumps up wondering if the chickens have been fed. So he opens the window and throws feed out to them. He just gets back to his letter when Leander enters, wishing to speak to Vielgeschrey about the possibility of marrying Leonora, Vielgeschrey's daughter.

Vielgeschrey tells Leander how busy he is and bids him to say what he has to say as quickly as possible and then leave. But before Leander can get one word out, a barber enters. Vielgeschrey's conversation and letter are dropped immediately, and he tells the barber to shave him as quickly as possible. He is no sooner lathered up when a farmer enters and Vielgeschrey is off doing business with him. During this, a tailor enters to begin measuring Vielgeschrey for a new suit of clothes. In the confusion the farmer gets by with paying Vielgeschrey only two-thirds of his debt. Suddenly Vielgeschrey notices that the lather is drying on his face, so he runs back to the barber. During his shave he must be reintroduced to Leander because he has forgotten why the young man came to see him. There is just enough time for Vielgeschrey to turn down Leander's proposal because he will accept as a son-in-law only a bookkeeper who can help him keep his affairs in order.

Royal Danish Theatre production of *Mascarade* in 1954, with Holgar Gabrielsen as "Leonard" and Pøul Reumert as "Jeronimus."

Photograph by Rigmor Mydtskov
The Royal Danish Theatre's Archives

Royal Danish Theatre production of *The Fortunate Shipwreck* in 1974, with Jørgen Reenberg as "Rosiflengius," Bodil Kjer as "Magdelone," Ghita Nørby as "Pernille," and Birthe Nieumann as "Leonora."

Photograph by Rigmor Mydtskov
The Royal Danish Theatre's Archives

Royal Danish Theatre production of *Jean de France* in 1976, with Paul Hüttel as "Pierre," Steen Springborg as "Jean," and Benny Hansen as "Arv."

Royal Danish Theatre production of *The Invisible Ladies* in 1978, with Peter Schrøder as "Harlekin," and Susse Wold as "The Invisible Lady."

The interior of Lille Grønnegade Theatre at the time of Holberg, as conceived by Rasmus Christiansen. Property of Teaterhistorisk Museum, The Royal Court Theatre, Copenhagen.

This humorous scene provides much opportunity for comic business with the barber oversoaping Vielgeschrey's face, the tailor trying to measure him while he runs about the stage, and the farmer swindling him. It also depicts his character trait very well. But it is the only scene in which the quirk is dramatized; the rest of the play involves the intrigue designed to unite Leonora and Leander in matrimony. Compared to *Jean de France*, little is done to exploit the foible. Granted, the intrigue is successful because of Vielgeschrey's foible, but it is designed primarily to help the young lovers rather than to satirize disorganization or false busyness. With the aid of disguises and Vielgeschrey's confusion, Leander and Leonora are united, while the bookkeeper intended for Leonora is married to another servant, Magdelone. When Vielgeschrey discovers that his daughter is not, in fact, married to a bookkeeper, he raises such a clamor that Leander promises to study bookkeeping. By pacifying Vielgeschrey, this ending actually encourages his ridiculous behavior.

In the plays other than character comedies, the stories are based almost exclusively upon situation; the characters merely react to what is happening. Characterization becomes more superficial, yet still funny and appealing. In *Diderich—Terror of Mankind*, for example, Leander has fallen in love with the beautiful Hyacinthe, a slave owned by Ephraim. Leander's stubborn father, Jeronimus, tells him to forget about the girl because she has already been sold to Diderich, an infamous officer. To thwart the sale, Leander's servant, Henrich, stages an intrigue, whereby Diderich's angered wife disguises herself as Hyacinthe. Henrich disguises himself as Ephraim and sells Diderich his own wife. Later Henrich disguises himself as an officer and takes delivery of the real Hyacinthe. Toward the end of the play, when everyone's disguise is removed and it seems the intrigue will fail, it is discovered that Hyacinthe is really Jeronimus's niece, Leonore, who was kidnapped years ago by barbarians. Leonore is therefore freed from bondage, and Diderich's wife beats him all the way home. As is typical of Holberg's non-character comedies, each character's actions are based solely upon his or her role in the situation. All that is ever learned about their personalities is related to their social position, age, and sex.

The above examples illustrate the frequent emphasis upon the foibles of the main characters in the Holberg comedies. If a character has an unusual trait, it has become ingrained in him before the play begins. Holberg also exaggerates the foibles being ridiculed, causing the characters to become caricatures rather than well-rounded individuals. As noted in chapter two, Holberg defended this exaggeration of character when answering his foreign critics. He believed that traits must be exaggerated to make the characters interesting and to provide the background for the comic intrigues ridiculing the various foibles. Even Holberg's most complex character, Jeppe, merely reacts to the extreme situations thrust upon him. The comedies contain no complex character studies, such as Molière's misanthrope, Alceste; rather, Holberg's characters resemble those drawn by Shakespeare in his earliest comedies, such as *Comedy of Errors*. Even in Holberg's philosophical comedies none of the characters wrestle with moral or philosophical issues, unexpected traits or behavior; each character has his viewpoint at the beginning of the play, and then circumstances verify one position while disproving the other. In other words , the characters in the philosophical comedies remain as unchanged as those in the other comedies.

For example, the issue of the effect of money on otherwise "good" individuals is examined in *Plutus*. Timotheus complains that Plutus, the god of wealth, is blind. The land in which they live is a very poor, but very good country with honest, hard-working, generous people (despite their meagre funds). Timotheus feels that they much more deserve to receive wealth than the rich countries surrounding them. These countries, he complains, are filled with evil, miserly, hard-hearted people. Timotheus's complaint reaches the ears of Jupiter, who decides to heal Plutus so that his gifts can be distributed more equitably. Upon learning this, Timotheus's friend Diogenes is outraged. He contends that their country's people are good *because* they are poor; when they receive money they will become like their neighbors. There is the crux of the play: who is right, Timotheus or Diogenes? But neither character has a particularly inquiring mind; just as in the character comedies, they begin the play with their opinions firmly established. The course of the play merely provides incidents to demonstrate which viewpoint is correct—in this case, Diogenes' theory that money will transform men into wicked, hard-hearted misers. At the play's conclusion, Timotheus concedes to Diogenes, but he never goes through the process of searching for the right answer as Hamlet does. There is no psychological development of character in Holberg's comedies.

Besides the main characters (the regular family members and servants) in the comedies, many incidental characters are used to comment upon the action or to make some sort of statement regarding the issues of the play. These characters usually appear on the stage very briefly, but they voice very specific opinions or show very particular traits. In order to make these statements and show these attitudes as quickly as possible, Holberg relies heavily upon stereotypes.

For example, in *The Maternity Room*, about twenty different people visit the exhausted new mother in her recovery room. These people run on with cock-and-bull stories, gossip, and arguments, often ignoring the mother they are supposedly visiting. Some of the characters have as few as three lines, but because they are stereotypes, they can make their point and exit without requiring significant character development.

In addition, Holberg uses a sort of second generation stereotype, in which he adds to the impact of the stereotype by reusing those he had already fleshed out in other plays. In these instances the audience reacts both to the stereotype and to their recollection of the humorous character from the other play. For instance, in *Witchcraft* it appears the Danish theatres will be closed. Several stereotypical characters cross the stage to voice their opinion of the closing, including a Dane affected by the French mode named Jean de France, an armchair politician named Herman von Bremen (*The Political Tinker*), and even von Quoten, leader of the German troupe which performed the bombastic sagas satirized in *Ulysses von Ithacia*. Holberg merely lifted all of these characters from his earlier scripts and from local personalities. When a person named Jean de France entered, the audience knew exactly who he was and what his personality was like. Their memory of him in the play *Jean de France* added to the impact of the stereotype.

COMIC CHARACTERS

If little else, Holberg's universal, typical characters are comic. No matter what the type of comedy or its subject matter—no matter what the social position, sex, or education of the individuals involved—Holberg's characters are humorous. Much of the fun of the plays springs from the actions and attitudes of the characters. They say and do funny things by accident and on purpose. Consider the following illustrations.

Jeppe, in *Jeppe of the Hill*, is an uneducated, lazy, drunken peasant whose wife beats him regularly. When he is introduced onto the stage, he is being beaten out of the house by his wife. When she leaves him alone he complains to the audience, explaining about his wife and his drinking:

JEPPE Now that sow's going in to eat breakfast, while I, miserable wretch, have to walk four miles to town without getting any food or drink. Can any man have such a damnable wife as mine? I really think she's the devil's own sister. Everyone in the country gossips about my drinking, but they never say why I drink. I get more beatings from that woman in one day than in my ten years in the militia! She beats me, the overseer whips me to work like a beast, and the deacon makes love to my wife behind my back. So why shouldn't I drink? Don't I have the right to use the means nature gave me to drive away my sorrows? If I was a fool such things wouldn't bother me and I wouldn't have to drink. But everyone knows I'm a bright man; I feel the pain more than others. So I have to drink. My friend, Moens Christoffersen, said to me, "The devil lives in your fat belly, Jeppe. If you stopped drinking, your wife wouldn't be so hard on you." I explained that I can't stop drinking for three reasons: First, I don't have the nerve. Second, that damned Mister Erich that hangs on the wall behind the bed. Third, and I don't say it out of conceit, I'm an even-tempered, Christian man who would never attempt to get revenge—not even against the deacon, who makes me hornier and hornier every day! Every holiday I pay a good offering to that man, and he never invites me in for a glass of beer! And nothing ever hurt me more than what he said a couple of years ago. I was telling some friends about a bull who had never feared any man, excepting for me. He cracked, "Don't you get it, Jeppe? The bull saw that your horns were bigger than his! He didn't want to fight his superior!" Don't you think, good people, that these things can drive an honorable man to drink? And even with all her faults, I've never once wished any evil to befall my wife. Once, when she was very sick with jaundice, I even prayed for her recovery. After all, hell is already full of evil women. If she dies, Lucifer might send her back and then she'd be even worse!   [act 1, scene 3]

The major source of comedy in Jeppe's monologue is his personality. Here is a very undesirable person— drunken, lazy, and not too bright—attempting to justify his faults. Though he is perfectly serious, his justifications are comical. Here is a man being cuckolded by the deacon, but is he angry with the deacon because of that? No. Jeppe is angry with him because the deacon will not give him a glass of beer when he pays his offerings. He does not care that the deacon is making love to his wife, but he cares that he is too cheap to offer him a glass of beer. When the audience sees the type of person Jeppe is, and then hears Jeppe's account of himself, the incongruity is funny. The humor in this scene arises not from true wit, which is intentional with the character, but from the fact that Jeppe acts in a ludicrous and unexpected way. He is not trying to be amusing, but his attitudes are amusing. He is funny to us, but not to himself.

The following scene from *Erasmus Montanus* also depicts comedy springing from character. In this scene, Erasmus Montanus, a sophomoric student, demonstrates his newly acquired ability to make logical deductions:

ERASMUS   I'll turn you into a stone, Mother.

NILLE   What talk! I'd like to see you try!

ERASMUS   Just listen. A stone cannot fly.

NILLE   That's true enough, unless someone throws it.

ERASMUS   You cannot fly.

NILLE   That's true.

ERASMUS   *Ergo*, you, Little Mother, are a stone.
　　(*Nille begins to cry.*)
　　Why are you crying, Mother?

NILLE   I'm afraid to be a stone! My legs are already beginning to get cold.

ERASMUS   Don't worry, Little Mother. I can turn you into a person again just as quickly. A stone can neither think nor talk.

NILLE   That's true. I don't know if it can think, but it can't talk.

ERASMUS   But you can talk.

NILLE   Yes, thank God, I can talk as well as a poor farmer's wife can.

ERASMUS *Ergo*, Little Mother is not a stone.
NILLE Oh good! I'm beginning to feel like myself again. It takes a strong head to study. I don't see how your brain can hold out.   [act II, scene 3]

Both characters in the scene add to the comedy. Erasmus is comic because he actually believes he is an expert in logical deduction. Nille is funny because she actually believes the deductions Erasmus makes are true. Neither of their beliefs reflects reality; therefore they are incongruous and funny.

Besides inventing characters who are unintentionally funny, such as Jeppe, Erasmus, and Nille, Holberg also invented characters conscious of their humor. Chilian, in *Ulysses von Ithacia*, makes sarcastic and humorous observations about the action of the play directly to the audience:

CHILIAN Now, after a whole year I've returned to my fatherland. That year surely went by fast! It didn't even seem like half an hour to me. But there's my master, still sitting there asleep. Good grief! He certainly grew that beard quickly! Oh yes, I forgot, he had a whole year in which to grow it. But my beard didn't grow at all. Maybe beards don't grow as fast in other countries as they do here. (*He feels Ulysses' beard.*) What the hell! It isn't even attached! (*He picks up the beard and holds it in front of his own face.*) Now, my friends, you can see that I've been away for a whole year. You're so sceptical, you wouldn't have believed it if I hadn't proved it to you.   [act I, scene 14]

Chilian intentionally ridicules the inconsistensies of the German saga's use of time. He makes an issue out of one character's beard growing and not his own, even though the same amount of time supposedly had passed for both of them. All through *Ulysses von Ithacia*, Chilian turns to the audience and sarcastically remarks about both the conventions of the German sagas and the action of the play. He is funny to the audience, and he knows that he is being funny.

Holberg created characters that are comic both because of incongruity and because they are witty. No matter what the social position or background of his characters, Holberg usually was able to delineate them in a comic way. Because his characters are universal, they have retained their humor through the years. The use of universal stock characters does not demonstrate any great characterizing interest or skill, but it shows a sensitivity to basic human nature and an understanding of the power that familiar types have on an audience. This skill in choosing a character is important. When an audience thinks, "Yes, I've seen that person somewhere!" the character tends to work. The most popular Holberg characters are those who are most universal—that is, types most familiar to Western audiences from everyday experience. Erasmus Montanus, the sophomoric student; Vielgeschrey, the busy man; Herman von Bremen, the armchair politician; and Jean de France, the person who rejects his own home for the "greener grass" over the hill, are all popular characters in terms of the number of performances their plays have had at the Royal Danish Theatre. On the other hand, unpopular characters have been Polidor, the alchemist in *The Arabian Powder*; Sganarel in *Sganarel's Travels to the Philosophical Land*; and Diogenes in *Plutus*. None of these characters possesses a universal quality. Polidor was popular for a short time in

Denmark, but when alchemy was outdated, his character became outdated. Sganarel and Diogenes are both "philosophical" characters of one type or another; they are vehicles to express some of Holberg's personal opinions about philosophers and are therefore not universal. In Holberg's most successful plays, the comic nature of the characters combined with their universal appeal provides a strong foundation for the plays' continuing popularity.

FIVE

Dialogue

HOLBERG, LIKE MOST PLAYWRIGHTS, depends almost wholly upon dialogue to tell his stories and to delineate his characters. Even though his characters tend to speak everyday eighteenth-century Copenhagen Danish regardless of their sex or social station, variations in language are used in some instances to enhance personalities, individualize scripts, and provide humor. This chapter will examine Holberg's use of dialogue.

LINGUISTIC INDIVIDUATION

One of the basic devices used by dramatists to show differences between characters and within characters is the individualization of their dialogue. For example, some characters might choose different types of words than others; differences in sentence structure from character to character might mean something; a character's use of prose or poetry, or even the overall length of his speeches might provide insights into his personality. In the same manner, a playwright may individualize moments within scripts, or even entire scripts, through the thoughtful use of this technique. A playwright's use of linguistic individuation can provide subtle insight into the characters, scenes, and scripts he has created. Some writers, such as Homer and Shakespeare, have used it so well that matters of authorship have been determined by it. Other dramatists almost ignore the differences in people's speech except in the most blatant circumstances. Holberg is one of the latter. What use Holberg does make of individuation through language for characters, moments, and scripts will now be examined.

Individualization of Personality

An examination of Holberg's dialogue indicates that, almost without exception, characters speak in the common, Copenhagen Danish of the early eighteenth century. Probably because of the speed with which Holberg wrote, all of his characters tend to use the same diction, syntax, and even imagery. It is a safe assumption that Holberg simply delineated characters by name, position, sex, and attitude and then used his own daily speech as a pattern for their expression. Servants and masters, young and old, upper and lower classes, males and females, farmers and city dwellers—all use the same speech throughout most of the comedies. For example, if a character wishes ill fortune on another, he says, "I hope you have an accident." If he threatens another with physical violence, he says, "I'll box your ears!" If a character calls someone a name, it is most often a "snake." In some instances, however, Holberg does differentiate characters through their speech. He uses limited speech individualization with the character Niels Studenstrup in *The Eleventh of June*. He also delineates some personality traits with language, usually through the use of a foreign language in one way or another.

Two of Holberg's main characters, Niels Studenstrup and Jacob von Tyboe, are Jutlanders. The Jutland dialect is very different from the Copenhagen; even today it is not unusual for a Copenhagen television station to subtitle an interview with a person from some parts of Jutland. So, of all his Danish characters, it would seem most natural for Holberg to distinguish the Jutlanders in their dialogue. Such is the case, but to a very limited degree. Jacob von Tyboe is a braggart, and it was natural for Holberg to make him a Jutlander, since Jutlanders were already stereotyped by Copenhageners as braggarts. However, only one von Tyboe speech is even remotely Jutlandish. Niels Studenstrup, then, is the only Danish character in a Holberg comedy to be differentiated through dialect to some degree. His only true use of the Jutlandish dialect occurs just after his first entrance: he uses the Jutlandish expression *"a"* instead of *"Jeg"* for the pronoun, *"I."* Even this usage, however, is dispensed with after the character has spoken fewer than ten lines.

Studenstrup does go on to use occasional Jutlandish expressions. For example, he refuses to stay at an inn without paying in advance, "because I would be embarrassed by doing so." He really means that he will avoid being cheated by taking that precaution; the innkeeper might try to demand a higher price in the morning, which Studenstrup would be forced to pay if he did not pay in advance. The usual Copenhagener would simply say, "I'll pay in advance so he won't be able to cheat me." Studenstrup is careful with his money because it "is not a thing to joke with in these times." A Copenhagener would say, "It is hard to come by these days." And, when being emphatic, Studenstrup uses the Jutlandish double reference to himself: "That must be understood by *Niels Studenstrup* and *me.*" The phrasing would seem to mean that "Niels Studenstrup" and "me" are two different people, but it actually reinforces the fact that "I, Niels Studenstrup, must understand that." This is also the only Jutlandish expression that Jacob von Tyboe uses ("*Jacob von Tyboe* and *I* have to take the entire army on our consciences").

These instances comprise Holberg's use of Danish dialects in the comedies. Even though these characters and some other minor Holberg characters are Jutlandish, and even though several of the comedies' characters are from Zealand farms, where another dialect is spoken, the dialects are simply not written into the scripts. However, Danish actors customarily apply the various appropriate dialects to the characters when they perform the plays. Since this tradition is known to have existed for over two hundred years, it is likely that the actors also applied the correct dialects to the characters during the time of Holberg. Indeed, Holberg in his autobiography praises an actor who performed Jeppe with the perfect illusion of a Zealand peasant; surely this characterization included the appropriate dialect. But the point remains that such a performance is a matter of application, and not a matter of using a playwright's written dialect as a guide, as it is in such plays as Sean O'Casey's *Juno and the Paycock.*

The only standard Copenhagen character in Holberg's comedies to be individualized by his speech is Rosiflengius in *The Fortunate Shipwreck*. Rosiflengius is a flatterer, so when he is speaking to people he hopes to impress, he uses overly picturesque words and hoary clichés:

ROSIFLENGIUS It is thy good mercy, not my own doing, that has opened the way to such joy. I do hope that your dear seedling, I mean your virgin daughter, will find joy with such a man as I. I have not inherited any wealth from my dear parents, but I thank them and kiss their memory for the fine education and upbringing they gave me. In my green youth they taught me the things with which I can earn my bread. Yea, I was barely two times eight winters old before I could write verse . . . and now, not a day passes in which I do not earn at least ten rixdaler through my writing. [act I, scene 6]

Alone with his servant, however, Rosiflengius uses everyday Copenhagen speech:

ROSIFLENGIUS You get home. If anyone desiring a wedding verse comes while I'm gone, you can just take one out of the third drawer. It doesn't matter which one you take. Do the same with eulogy verses; they're in the fifth drawer. And for advancements in position and status, take a verse from the fourth drawer. [act IV, scene 3]

Rosiflengius is the only character in the Holberg comedies who uses different language for different purposes. His character defect is demonstrated through his language, which varies according to his audience and his purpose. This particular trait could not have been adequately demonstrated in any other way; in order to show

Rosiflengius's hypocritical character, Holberg *had* to use two types of vocabulary. Therefore, this difference does not imply subtle nuances of character, but serves to demonstrate the given foible.

Foreign languages in Holberg's comedies are also used as a method to indicate personality. But, as with the overly picturesque vocabulary of Rosiflengius, this type of linguistic individuation is simply necessary to reveal a character's quirk or foible. Usually when one of Holberg's characters uses a foreign language, he speaks *at* the language rather than speaking it correctly. For example, consider the way Hans Frandsen (Jean de France) speaks French; he believes he speaks it well, but his comic misuse of French is a glaring demonstration of his foible.

Characters in *Erasmus Montanus* treat Latin in almost the same way. In this play, Rasmus Berg has just returned home from the university. He has Latinized his name and shows off by dropping Latin phrases into his speech whenever possible. Not to be outdone, Per Degn, the local schoolmaster, brags about his knowledge of Latin. Unfortunately, it has been years since Per studied Latin and he remembers very little. Here he explains a few things about Latin to Erasmus's family:

NILLE   I sliced some bread and cheese, if you want any.
PER   Thank you, Little Mother. Do you know what "bread" is called in Latin?
NILLE   I have no idea.
PER   It's called *Panis, genetivus Pani, dativus Pano, vocativus Panus, ablativus Pano.*
JEPPE   Good heavens! that language is long-winded. What is the name for coarse bread?
PER   It's called *Panis gravis* and fine bread is *Panis finis.*

JEPPE   Why, that's half Danish!

PER   That's right. There are many Latin words that have their origin in Danish. Let me explain. There is an old school teacher in Copenhagen named Saxo Grammatica, who is responsible for improving Latin here in this country. He also wrote a Latin grammar book. That's how he got the name, Saxo Grammatica. This same man has introduced many Danish words into the Latin. Before he did that, Latin was such a poor language that it was impossible to express a thought correctly in it.   [act I, scene 4]

Later in the play, Erasmus (Rasmus Berg) and Per Degn have a disputation in Latin. Erasmus has learned his Latin well, while Per's is terrible; he can only remember some isolated words and lists. But the local villagers do not know that, and Per makes the best of their ignorance:

PER   Who is the *imprimatur* this year?

ERASMUS   What does that mean?

PER   I mean, who is the *imprimatur* to the poems and books that go to the printers?

ERASMUS   Is that supposed to be Latin?

PER   Yes. In my time it was good Latin.

ERASMUS   If it was good Latin then, it should be good Latin now. And as far as I know, that isn't Latin the way you are using it.

PER   Well, I say that it *is* good Latin.

ERASMUS   Is it a *Nomen* or a *Verbum*?

PER   It's a *Nomen*.

JESPER   That's right, Per! You tell him!

ERASMUS   *Cujus declinationis*, is that *imprimatur*?

PER   All of the words you have used are one of eight things: *Nomen*, *Pronomen*, *Verbum*, *Princi pium*, *Conjugatio*, *Declinatio*, or *Interjectio*.

JESPER   Just listen to Per when he shakes his armor! That's right!

ERASMUS   He hasn't answered anything I've asked him! What is *Imprimatur* in *Genitivo*?

PER   *Nominativus Ala, Genituivus Alae, Dativus Alo, Vocativus Alo, Ablativus Ala.*

JESPER   There you have it, Monsieur Montanus! We also have educated people out here in the country! [act III, scene 3]

So the use and misuse of Latin in *Erasmus Montanus* is essential to establishing personality in both Rasmus Berg (Erasmus) and Per Degn. It demonstrates Erasmus's sophomoric pedantry and reveals Per's foolish self-importance, as he purposefully misuses Latin knowing that his uneducated friends will accept anything he says. Nevertheless, except for this use and misuse of Latin, the language of the characters is the same as that of the other Holberg characters—everyday Copenhagen prose.

In both *Erasmus Montanus* and *Jean de France*, the foibles could not be depicted nearly so well without the misuse of a foreign language. Certainly Erasmus displays his foible in other ways, such as attempting to turn his mother into a stone through the misuse of logical deductions. Likewise, the pretentious Jean carries out every absurd order Madame La Flèche gives him simply because he believes her to be describing the latest French modes. But the misuse of a foreign language is the primary character device in these two plays. And because of that misuse, the other foible-revealing incidents become more pointed.

Holberg also uses foreign languages in other, less significant ways. For example, two of his characters, Jeppe and Jacob von Tyboe, have served in the militia. In Holberg's time, orders in the militia were given in German. So, both characters speak *at* German when trying to impress those around them. Here Jacob von Tyboe explains what happens when a man falls in love: "When Venus says to her son, Cupid, '*Stellet Euer Gewehr sur Ladung* (Hold your rifles, open the pan),' even the strongest of men must tremble" [act III, scene 5]. And in *Jeppe of the Hill*, Jeppe explains why he knows some German:

JEPPE *Ich tank ju* (I thank you), Jacob.
JACOB I hear that you speak German, Jeppe!
JEPPE Yes, but only when I'm drunk.
JACOB Then you must speak it at least once a day.
JEPPE I was in the militia ten years, shouldn't I recognize my own speech?   [act I, scene 6]

This use of German by Jacob von Tyboe and Jeppe is a minor, humorous facet which better defines their personalities. It works primarily as a comic device, though, not to provide subtle insights into their characters.

One other Holberg character uses a foreign language; in *The Fortunate Shipwreck*, Henrich speaks at Dutch in order to cause the misunderstanding on which the intrigue is based. By doing so Henrich demonstrates that he must have spent some time on the docks of Copenhagen, but the purpose of the Dutch is to bring about the misunderstanding and not to reveal anything about his personality. Here Henrich sets in motion the intrigue that will expose Rosiflengius's true avaricious motives in his flattery and courtship of Leonora:

PERNILLE Oh! What an unfortunate accident!
JERONIMUS What is it?
PERNILLE I can't say it. There's a sailor outside, let him say it.

JERONIMUS   The word "sailor" kills me! I'm afraid something
has happened to my ship. Let him come in!
HENRICH   (*Enters disguised as a Dutch sailor.*)
Myn Heer! ick breng Jouw een zeer bedroeft Tydung. (My
lord! I bring you very terrible news.)
MAGDELONE   My whole body is shaking!
JERONIMUS   What is it?
HENRICH   *Myn Heer heft syn Scheep verloeren.* (My Lord has
lost his ship.)
JERONIMUS   What! My ship sunk?
HENRICH   *Wel ja, myn Heer! Vor sess Dagen ist die Onglyck
gearriveert.* (Yes, my lord! It happened six days ago.)
JERONIMUS   (*Crying.*) Where did it happen?
HENRICH   *In Cattegat, myn Heer. Tuschen twalf en een Uur
tegen Mitnacht.* (In Kattegat, my lord, between midnight
and one o'clock.)   [act IV, scene 4]

Henrich's Dutch, while not completely correct, is
probably the type of Dutch-Danish a Dutch sailor would
try to speak in Copenhagen during the eighteenth century. It is Dutch enough for the effect, yet comprehensi-
ble enough for the Copenhagen audience.

Thus, Holberg individualized the language of his
characters in very limited ways. Even when writing the
dialogue for characters who would normally speak dialects different from the standard Copenhagen Danish,
he did not indicate those dialects, with the minor exception of Niels Studenstrup's first lines in the *Eleventh of
June.* Holberg did individualize three major characters
through language: Rosiflengius, Jean de France, and Erasmus Montanus; depiction of these characters' foibles depends upon specific language differentiations of one kind
or another. Secondly, Holberg used German as a minor
device in *Jeppe of the Hill* and *Jacob von Tyboe* to sup-

port the revealed nature of the characters' foibles. Finally, he used a foreign language to cause the misunderstanding on which the intrigue is based in *The Fortunate Shipwreck*.

Individualization of Moments

Playwrights often individualize dialogue to subtly differentiate various moments within a script. Shakespeare was a master of this technique. In *Richard II*, for example, the imagery of the setting and rising sun is carefully used throughout the script to indicate the changing relationship between Richard and Bolingbroke as King Richard loses power and abdicates, and Bolingbroke becomes King Henry IV. The fact that Holberg did not make use of this technique does not mean that his scripts are inferior; they simply do not include this particular dimension of expression. Considering that the characters in the comedies are the same at the end of the plays as they are at the beginning, having experienced no inner change or shifts in attitude with the occasional exception of some characters having overcome their foibles, it is understandable that no such individualization of moments was necessary.

Individualization of Scripts

Holberg uses language individuation to differentiate two of his scripts from all of the others. These are the two dramatic satires, *Ulysses von Ithacia* and *Melampe*.

In *Ulysses von Ithacia*, Holberg satirizes the bombastic German sagas performed in Copenhagen during

the earliest years of the eighteenth century by von Quoten's acting troupe. To exaggerate his satire, Holberg uses
stiff, formal language for the general's and aristocrats' dialogue. (As usual, the servants speak everyday Danish.) In
this example, Ulysses has just awakened from a deep
sleep:

ULYSSES   Oh, thou gods! I am aware that my dream has been
    fulfilled! I dreamt that the winged god, Mercury, came to
    me, declaring these words, "Thy true servant, Chilian, has
    returned, removing thy unkempt beard." (*He sees Chi-
    lian*.) Now I see him. Welcome thou loyal servant! I doubt
    not that thine errand has been successfully fulfilled. Yea,
    the heavens have guided thee in thy travels!

[act I, scene 14]

Ulysses's speech in *Ulysses von Ithacia* does set him
apart as a general among the other characters. But Holberg did not intend these stiff, formal speeches to illumi-
nate Ulysses's character; they comprise a specific satirical point directed at the language used in the German
sagas. Just as the vocabularies of Jean de France and Rosiflengius must be differentiated to clarify their foibles, the
language of Ulysses must be stiff and formal to satirize
the German plays.

Similarly, linguistic individuation in *Melampe* serves
to point up the satire of its dramatic form rather than to
demonstrate character traits. Holberg deliberately belit-
tles what he considered the ridiculousness of characters
speaking in verse in high tragedy, by having the aristocratic characters in *Melampe* speak in anguishing alexandrine verse. Only in this play do any of Holberg's char-

acters speak to one another in verse. (The commoners in *Melampe* speak ordinary Copenhagen Danish.) The following speech, so formal and pompous, becomes even more ludicrous when Melampe, the object of the wailing, is discovered to be a lap dog!

PHILOCYNE   Ah Philocyne! Thine only comfort is to mourn.
     Thine heart's delight has vanished, from thy bosom torn.
       Bliss and joy and happiness forevermore be thwarted.
       What could make me happy now? Melampe is departed.
     What balm is there for my poor heart's anguish?
     Reason crumbles while in pain I languish.
       All art and learning are with every joy aborted.
       For aught can lift my sorrow when Melampe is
       departed.
     In vain I devour volumes of philosophy
     In hopes some magic will reverse this catastrophe.
       I search and weep. Such teachings I've discarded
       For nothing can absolve my grief, Melampe is departed.
     Not friend, nor harps, nor books shall yet forbear
     To rid me of my monstrous black despair.
       I bravely sing and laugh, although I'm most down-
       hearted.
       My soul is rent; my heart's lament: Melampe is
       departed.
                          [act II, scene 3]

Although Holberg's use of alexandrine verse differentiates *Melampe* from his other plays, the characters who speak in verse all use the same sort of words, sentence structure, and imagery. So the aristocratic characters in *Melampe* are as similar to each other as the Copenhagen characters are to one another in the other comedies.

Holberg's use of individuation in *Ulysses von Ithacia* and *Melampe*—like his use of the device to reveal the
foibles of some of his characters—serves a necessary purpose. Had he attempted to lampoon the German sagas or
high tragedy without imitating their language, his satires
would probably have failed. But by satirizing the language
of these other dramatic forms, the entire scope of the satire is clear and easily understood by the audience. In
Holberg's scripts, although linguistic individuation gives
some insights into the personalities of those who speak
differently, its ultimate purpose is always to clarify some
point of the satire, not to show depth of character.

An examination of Holberg's scripts reveals that
most of his characters speak alike. This sameness of
speech is most evident in the scripts which are not set in
Copenhagen. It is easier to differentiate a dialect than
subtle differences of personality, but even when Holberg's
characters do not come from or live in Copenhagen, they
speak Copenhagen Danish. For example, *The Political
Tinker* is set in Hamburg, Germany, but it is impossible
to distinguish its characters from the Copenhageners in
Holberg's other comedies, as Rosenstand-Goiske noted in
his review of *The Political Tinker* in 1771. In like manner, *Don Ranudo* takes place in Spain, but the characters
speak Copenhagen Danish.

Holberg's plays also include Danish characters from
areas of Denmark other than Copenhagen. Jeppe, Erasmus Montanus, and the peasant boy in *The Peasant Boy
in Pawn* all come from Zealand farms; *Erasmus Montanus* actually takes place in a Zealand farmhouse. Zealand has an obvious dialect of its own, but the characters'

speeches are written in the Copenhagen dialect. One of the most striking examples of this lack of character individualization in the farmer comedies is found in *The Peasant Boy in Pawn*, in which the boy is a country rube. Even though an actor playing the role might use a Zealand dialect, the part is written in the same language as the Copenhageners'.

PERNILLE   Look at that peasant boy standing over there gaping. He must not have ever been in the city before.

LEERBEUTEL   Hey! Country boy! Where are you from?

PEASANT   I'm from a little town out in the country.

LEERBEUTEL   What's the town's name?

PEASANT   (*Thinks.*) I don't know.

LEERBEUTEL   Well, how far is it from here?

PEASANT   You mean from this city here?

LEERBEUTEL   What an idiot! You think I'm going to ask you how far the town is from where you're standing? You don't know the name of the town you live in? What's the name of your mayor? If you tell me his name I might be able to figure out where you live.

PEASANT   Our mayor? Let me see. He has the same name as me.

LEERBEUTEL   Then what's your name?

PEASANT   I can't remember. Let me see. Just a minute, I'm sure my mother knows it.   [act I, scene 3]

Since Holberg did not take the opportunity to linguistically delineate even such a vastly different character as the peasant boy from his other characters, it is obvious that he did not concern himself with language differentiation except in limited usages where it was demanded by the satire. For the most part, the characters' language does not reflect or reveal their sex, education, social position, or personality.

OTHER LINGUISTIC DEVICES

Besides standard dialogue between individuals, Holberg uses several other linguistic devices. Verse, monologues, and asides serve to reveal characters' motivation, to comment upon situations, to moralize at the end of plays, and to provide humor.

Verse

Holberg ended several of his character comedies with a poem to drive home the lesson being taught in the story. This closing poem is from *The Political Tinker*:

HERMAN   We oft condemn a leader's part,
  But we stand ineffectual;
  'Tis ease to read an ocean chart,
  But not to steer a vessel.

  From a book on politics
   We can learn to reason.
  To know a country, how it ticks,
   Needs wisdom, though, well seasoned.

  Each working man should recognize
   From watching this diversion;
  Though he may leaders criticize,
   He knows not how to govern.

  A tinker cannot best perform
   As mayor by instinct, nor

Can a statesman quick transform
Himself into a tinker.

Holberg's characters speak in verse only in *Melampe*.
Any other time poetry appears in the comedies, it is an
epilogue, such as the above, or a poem recited by a character, usually in the interests of young love.

Two Holberg characters write bad poems that rein-
force the audience's awareness of their personalities.
Jeppe's poem is actually a series of lines which hardly
make sense. At the end of each line Jeppe alternates the
nonsense names "Peteheia" and "Polemeia" in order to
force a rhyme. The last four lines are enough of a sample:

JEPPE   I sat down on my steel grey horse, Peteheia!
The deacon is a roguish beast, Polemeia!
If you will know my wife's name, Peteheia!
She is called: shame and burden, Polemeia! [act I, scene 6]

The poem does not give any subtle clues into Jeppe's personality, but it reinforces our previous knowledge of him
as a lazy, drunken, uneducated braggart.

The second "poet" is Jacob Berg, brother of Erasmus
Montanus. Jacob is a popular, witty farm-boy. To prove
his wit to his pedantic brother, Jacob recites a comic epi-
taph he wrote for a man who drank himself to death:

JACOB   First you must know that both Morten's father and
grandfather were fishermen who drowned in water. The
verse goes like this:
Here lies Morten Nielsen,
In order to walk in his forefathers' footsteps,
Who drowned in water like fish,
Drowned himself in brandy.   [act IV, scene 4]

The meter is terrible, but the words are clever. The poem causes Erasmus to accept the fact that there are witty peasants; nevertheless, he bemoans the fact that Jacob does not want to become educated.

Thus, Holberg's incidental verse serves chiefly as moralization at the end of some of the character comedies. In addition, a young man is occasionally allowed to read a love poem, an especially bad poem was written for Jeppe as a bit of comic business supporting his established personality, and a clever but meterless verse was written for Jacob to sway his brother. Holberg's use of poetry *within* the plays serves only to support established personality traits.

The Monologue

Through the ages, the monologue has been one of the most popular linguistic devices used by playwrights. It draws the audience into the character's world. It often allows the audience to know things about the characters that none of the other persons on stage know. It can shorten exposition and allow the playwright to get on with the action. And it can be very funny. Holberg made extensive use of the monologue to set scenes, reveal characteristics and motivations, explain attitudes, and inform the audience of intrigues that are about to be sprung.

The monologue explaining motivation is typified by the long "Jeppe" monologue cited in chapter four, in which Jeppe comes forward to tell the audience why he drinks. Another shorter and much more blatant example of a monologue used to explain motivation occurs in *Without Head or Tail*, in which two old women have been exploiting fanatics who believe that every little thing is a sign from heaven. Through their dishonest means, Gunnild has secured a handsome young man, Leander, to become her daughter's husband. Marthe, her cohort, suddenly decides to expose Gunnild by going to Leander's brother and setting up a plan which will expose her phony practices. After the plan is arranged, Marthe explains her change of heart to the audience:

MARTHE (*Laughs.*) I'm actually not doing this either to free my conscience or to expose Gunnild's sins. I'm doing it because I'm bitter. I don't want to see Gunnild have such good luck which would earn honor and glory for her. I'm not the first woman ever to put herself in jeopardy and sabotage a friendship because of envy and spite. Envy is the strongest passion raging in a woman's heart. It can force a woman to jeopardize her own welfare, good name, family, friends, and position. After Gunnild is exposed and I'm paid for my services, I'll just move to another location and go into business for myself. But here they come, I have to go and prepare things.   [act IV, scene 9]

Chapter four cited a monologue from *The Busy Man* in which an individual's characteristics are explained— Pernille's explanation of her master's busyness. In this short excerpt of such a monologue from *The Fickle Woman*, Henrich describes his lady:

HENRICH If I continue my daily practice of always trying to answer my lady, I'll soon become a great lawyer whose finest attribute is the ability to compliment a thing, and then, in the next breath, to expound on the evils of that same thing. The only clock I need is my lady's mind. After she's changed her mind eight or ten times from bad-tempered, to pious, to blasphemous, to worldly, religious,

generous, miserly, noisy, quiet, humble, conceited, and so
on, then I know it's noon. . . .   [act I, scene 5]

In this speech from *The Fickle Woman* and in Pernille's
speech from *The Busy Man*, Holberg eliminates the need
for lengthy dialogue or action demonstrating the central
character's foible. By saving time in these two shorter
plays he can get right into the action. Also, while con-
serving time, he entertains his audience with the humor
in these monologues.

Another Henrich, in *Without Head or Tail*, uses the
monologue to explain his own attitudes to the spectators:

HENRICH   My master thinks that when he goes into the
masked ball I sit out here and sleep with the other lackies!
You can bet your life I don't! I always have my own costume along and go in and dance with the other people.
When everyone is wearing a mask, they are all equal to
one another. This evening I have appointments to meet
four different ladies at the ball! The first one is David
Skolemester's dry-nurse. She is always a perfect lady. And
she can dance the cross-step! The next is Henrich Ur-
tegaardsmand's daughter. She's so bawdy that she'll make
love to *any* masked man—as long as he can pay a reason-
able price. The third is Gertrud Faestedone's daughter and
the fourth is her cousin, Mammeselle Nille. She and I
have been practicing that new English dance, the castil-
lion, together. . . .   [act II, scene 5]

Yet another Henrich delivers a monologue to set the
scene for a play, explaining the entire situation in *Henrich and Pernille*:

HENRICH   (*Enters dressed as a cavalier.*)
(*Laughs.*) Everything is going perfectly! She's all set! What

can't these fine clothes do for a man? Honestly, I didn't have anything in mind other than fantasizing a little when I dressed up in my master's clothing. Now it's going just like the man who dressed up in a doctor's robes as a joke for his friends. Only by dressing up, the people made him into a real doctor! I've become a true gentleman. That dear young lady has really fallen for me. But what does that mean? I will advance in life from a lowly snake to a distinguished gentleman. The thing that is most important is that I can act properly and that none of the rough old servant traits show through. Yesterday I almost ruined everything. I ordered some men to unload my master's wagon and then almost went back to help them! The foreman noticed me and grinned. Then he asked where "His Grace" was going. I blushed, but quickly recovered by pretending I saw something wrong with the back end of the wagon. I went to the Assembly yesterday just to try to copy some of the better people's manners. There was a Frenchman I copied some things from, but I refuse to speak through my nose! He was very graceful and I learned to do this: (*He takes out a small mirror and carefully adjusts his wig.*) I certainly enjoy this life! I love myself! I can see why that young lady loves me!   [act I, scene I]

Since most schemes in the comedies are worked out by two or more characters, they are usually discussed or demonstrated to the audience. Occasionally, though, a scheme is perpetrated by only one major figure, who must then explain it to the audience in a monologue. For example, in *The Arabian Powder*, Oldfux explains how his scheme against Polidor will work:

OLDFUX   It's going beautifully! I'll let things work out for him for a couple more times so I can swindle him out of even more. Polidor won't go wrong anytime he comes with ten

rixdaler for a handful of powder to put in his pan. But
when he comes across with four thousand rixdaler, my
friend Andreas and I will vanish from Copenhagen, letting
him wonder where he can buy more Arabian powder!
(*Laughs.*) That's going to be funny when he sends out for
something that has never existed and learns that no one
else has ever heard of "Arabian Powder." I'm swindling
him out of four thousand rixdaler, but I'm also doing him
a favor. He should be grateful to me. He's going to learn so
much from this experience that he'll forsake his madness
and leave the job of gold making to other fools. Andreas
will get one-fourth of the money for his part in the deal.
He's been eager and dependable with his part of the bar-
gain. But here comes Polidor.   [act I, scene 9]

The searching monologue of mental anguish is not
to be found in Holberg's comedies. They contain nothing
like Hamlet's soliloquy; nowhere does a character wrestle with the question of whether to be or not to be. The
superficiality of Holberg's characters does not allow such
searching. Instead, they address the audience to explain
light-heartedly about different facets of the play. These
monologues heighten interest as the audience is taken
momentarily into the characters' world.

The Aside

Finally, Holberg uses the aside quite often in his
comedies to allow a character to make short, quick observations about the action or the other characters by con-
fiding in the audience. As with the monologue, the aside
explains motive and attitude as well as provides a source
of humor. The following example from *Ulysses von Itha-*

cia was selected because of its extensive use of the aside. Here Chilian lets the audience know exactly what he thinks of the situation when it looks as though he will have to be executed:

ULYSSES   My faithful servant, Chilian! Take this obstinate old man, bind him in golden chains, and incarcerate him!

CHILIAN   (*Aside.*) Where the hell am I going to find golden chains? Even if the general wanted to hang himself, there isn't anything but rope to use around here. Oh well, I'll use this rope for golden chains, it'll work as well as the rice stalk did for the olive branch.

TIRESIUS   Oh noble soldiers! Spare my life. I haven't refused to prophesy about the outcome of this war because of villainy or obstinance. My prophecy contains a terrible message that will horrify your entire army!

ULYSSES   Speak out freely. Do not spare us anything.

TIRESIUS   Since you have commanded me to speak out freely, I won't hold back anything. Troy cannot be taken, nor you return home in victory, unless the faithful servant of Ulysses, Chilian, is offered and slain for the entire army.

ULYSSES   Is that all? My true servant Chilian will gladly do that!

CHILIAN   (*Aside.*) Like hell I will.

ULYSSES   He will beg me to offer him up, if I know him.

CHILIAN   (*Aside.*) He may know the devil! I'd be crazy to do that.

ULYSSES   He will do it with pleasure!

CHILIAN   (*Aside.*) What talk! I'd rather see his entire army hang before I offered anyone my little finger!

[act III, scene 2]

This use of the aside allows for comedy to be interjected in an otherwise less comic scene. It has been used through the ages in this manner, and Holberg adapted the device well to his plays.

In *The Busy Man* the aside is used for a completely different reason: the intrigue has been rather complicated, and at one point the audience needs to know that the characters have not discovered the intrigue, but are still in a state of confusion. Madsen believes that his son is going to marry Vielgeschrey's daughter, while Vielgeschrey, who arranged the marriage between his daughter and Madsen's son, cannot remember ever having seen Madsen before. In the fourth scene of act three, Vielgeschrey is led to believe that Madsen's son has come to marry his housekeeper, Magdelone. In this conversation, Madsen believes he and Vielgeschrey are talking about Vielgeschrey's daughter; Vielgeschrey believes they are discussing Magdelone:

MADSEN   Perhaps your daughter is fixing her makeup.

VIELGESCHREY   (*Aside.*) Oh yes, that strange mortician's style. (*To Madsen.*) I believe so. She doesn't like to use much makeup, but she probably is prettying herself up a little.

MADSEN   I can see that you are fairly conservative yourself, so it's natural that your children would be, too.

VIELGESCHREY   (*Aside.*) Still using that unusual style! (*To Madsen.*) No one in my house is going to learn vanity from me.

MADSEN   There, you said it yourself.

VIELGESCHREY   Have I ever had the honor of speaking with you before?

MADSEN   (*Aside.*) His head is still in a fog. (*To Vielgeschrey.*) I notice that my lord always has his head full of business matters.

VIELGESCHREY   That's true! That's why I've chosen a young

man with bookkeeping talents to marry my daughter. I'll
be able to employ him myself.

MADSEN Thank you, I'm honored.

VIELGESCHREY (*Aside.*) Still using that formal mortician's
speech! (*To Pernille.*) He's carrying on as though he's met
me before.

MADSEN (*Aside.*) Still in a fog. (*To Vielgeschrey.*) But here
comes the bride. (*To the others.*) There you have her, gentlemen, his dear daughter.

VIELGESCHREY (*Aside.*) I wish to hell he'd stop using those ridiculous mortician's expressions!   [act III, scene 4]

The gimmick is possibly overused in this scene.
However, the asides demonstrate that the characters have
not discovered the intrigue. And the intrigue succeeds;
Madsen believes his son is marrying Vielgeschrey's daughter, and Vielgeschrey marries off his housekeeper to the
man he wished to be his own son-in-law.

These two examples of the aside are unusual in that
they are longer and more involved than the usual Holberg
aside, which is usually a "throwaway"—that is, a short
comment by one character about another. The most common asides, found in all of his comedies, are the throw-
aways; they are usually calculated to get a laugh, as in
this example from *The Fortunate Shipwreck*:

ROSIFLENGIUS Don't cry, my goddess! The winged god, Cupid,
has inflicted you with a terrible love, that has until now
resided with the swan-carried goddess, Venus. She has ordered you smitten again so you can come to your senses.

PERNILLE (*Aside.*) That's the devil's own speech! If I ever said a
sentence like that, I'd throw up my entire lunch!

[act I, scene 6]

Thus, Holberg uses the aside to explain motives and feelings as well as to keep the story straight, as in *The Busy Man*. He also uses it as a fine comic tool. He has again, as in so many instances, been able to discern what devices in other plays have been successful and to use them to his own advantage.

Humor Based Upon Dialogue

Besides using the characters' words to convey their thoughts to each other and the audience, Holberg is a master at using dialogue to get a laugh. He is very adept at creating comic situations and then using them as vehicles for jokes. *The Maternity Room* provides a fine example of this. The new mother has been receiving visitors all day and is very tired. She has become somewhat sarcastic to some of her guests. When Arianche Bogtrykkers (Mrs. Bookprinter) enters, the conversation builds from several small jokes, as the women bounce comebacks off each other's remarks, to one grand punchline based upon the entire conversation:

MOTHER My husband enjoys reading very much. He's always buying new books. Yesterday he bought *Doctor Arendt Hvitfeld's Chronicles.*

ARIANCHE Which edition?

MOTHER The Danish edition.

ARIANCHE Is it the *quarto* or folio edition?

MOTHER It's the one in white.

ARIANCHE A printer can bind a book in ten different bindings if he wants to. I'm not interested in that. Don't you know what a folio is?

MOTHER The only folios I know of are fools in folios.

ARIANCHE (*Laughs.*) I've heard enough. You obviously don't know anything about books. A book in folio is as large as a Bible, a book in *quarto* is smaller, and a book in *octavo* is even smaller than those. *Duodece* is very small, and the smallest is the *sedece*.

MOTHER Then the book must be in folio because it's as large as a Bible.

ARIANCHE Madam! That edition isn't worth anything! Why don't you ask my husband's advice before you buy your books? The edition in *quarto* is much better.

MOTHER If that's true, it's the printer's fault! After all, it's a brand new book.

ARIANCHE (*Laughs.*)

MOTHER What are you laughing at? Maybe I don't speak just right. After all, I don't know anything about your business. Thank you for what you taught me. Now I know what a book in folio is. But let's talk about something else. Did you see the two women leaving as you came in?

ARIANCHE Yes.

MOTHER All they did was gossip! The one was Ingeborg Blytækkers and the other was Anne Kandestøbers.

ARIANCHE Which one was Anne Kandestøbers, the big or the little?

MOTHER The one in *quarto* is Ingeborg Blytækkers and the one in folio is Anne Kandestøbers.   [act II, scene 6]

Here, Holberg peppered the scene with some minor jokes, such as "Which edition?"—"The Danish edition," as he sets up the main punchline, "The one in *quarto* is Ingeborg Blytækkers and the one in folio is Anne Kandestøbers." The two women typify Holberg's middle-class audience, and he used the situation as the background for his humor.

The success of Holberg's comedies does not lie in a rich variety of linguistic devices or in his eloquence. Indeed, dialogue is a major source of the superficiality, the stereotypic quality of the characters in the Holberg comedies; it demonstrates their earthiness, not complexity or depth. Holberg was, however, a very able gagsmith, and his ability to write jokes is one of the main reasons for the success of the comedies. He was able to construct jokes based upon and illuminating his characters and their situations, so the humor remains fresh and timely. Had he used many topical jokes, just thrown in for extra laughs, as jokes often were in early American musicals, the appeal of the plays would have diminished through the years. Certainly the universal appeal of Holberg's humor is one of the factors that has enabled his comedies to remain popular for so long.

SIX

Comic Situations and Stage Activity

IT HAS ALREADY BEEN DEMONSTRATED that Holberg used comic characters and jokes to provoke laughter. But the stories and situations providing the background for those characters and jokes should also be amusing. On the topic of inciting laughter, J. W. Lange remarks that "there exist such things as *objects of universal laughter*, things which appeal to the sense of humor in every human intellect, which lightly upset the sense of propriety and order that is present in every human mind, and awaken laughter by their suddenness."[1] He goes on to cite comic devices that are universal, from Plautus to George M. Cohan: "ludicrous characterization, unexpected situations, mistaken identity, the discernment of difficulty and clumsiness, relief from a great strain, the mechanical and the stupid, suggestiveness, loss of dignity, perception of incongruity, turning on masters, and mimicry."[2] Holberg uses each of these devices to a greater or lesser degree. He was a master at creating comic situations that provide an excellent framework for his comic characters, intrigues, and funny business.

SITUATION

It is difficult for funny characters to sustain a comedy alone; they must have funny things to do. It is also difficult for jokes alone to sustain a comedy. In Holberg's plays the essential comic situation is the foundation for all the other elements of the play: characters, plot devices such as intrigues, and comic business. Consider the following typical Holberg situations:

In *The Fortunate Shipwreck,* a young lady's parents are deceived by a middle-aged flatterer and wish to marry her off to him instead of to the young man she loves. The flatterer is not only middle-aged, he is a hunchback.

In *Witchcraft,* a band of actors overheard rehearsing a play about witchcraft is mistaken for a coven of witches. While the townspeople speak publicly about destroying the "witches," they secretly come one by one to have their futures predicted or warts removed.

In *The Maternity Room,* an old man sires a baby with his young wife. Rumors abound that he has been cuckolded, so he hides in his wife's recovery room to learn if she has a young lover. A visitor to the maternity room notices a man hiding in the closet. Rumors of this new "proof" run rampant and eventually come back to the old husband, who is now sure that he has been cuckolded—until he discovers that the man in hiding was none other than himself.

In *The Christmas Room,* a young woman married to

an old man has fallen in love with a young man. She holds a rendezvous with her young lover in the room decorated for Christmas. It is the maid's job to keep the old man out of the Christmas room while the rendezvous takes place. Of course, he eventually discovers the lovers.

Holberg's plays are situation comedies. Sometimes the takeoff is a foible; other times it is a predicament. The main source of fun is what happens on the surface. This surface structure is perhaps not so profound as psychological or social development in a character, but the plays are not superficial or uninteresting as a result. Holberg's clever comic situations provide the foundation for the rest of the comic devices within each play. These basic situations have retained their humor for more than two hundred years. Not surprisingly, they are as universal as the characters. Holberg borrowed situations from other playwrights; but by adapting these situations to his own story lines, by giving them Danish locales, and by using them to satirize human faults, he made them his own. They were new to his audience. Even today these situations can appear fresh, and not borrowed from antiquity, when placed in modern settings. In fact, they resemble many situation comedies on television.

The Intrigue

Holberg's most often used plot device is the intrigue, a misrepresentation accomplished through disguise to cause a victim to make a certain decision or perform a certain action. Twenty-six of the thirty-three comedies contain intrigues, which usually serve the purpose of exposing a character's foible and/or uniting young lovers.

Occasionally the intrigue is no more than a scheme designed to swindle money or possessions from the unwary, as in *Abracadabra*. Some of the intrigues are simple, other are incredibly complex; some are logical, others are totally preposterous. No matter what form an intrigue takes, Holberg sets it up masterfully and exploits it in several comic ways.

Intrigues have already been explained in detail throughout this study to support various other hypotheses: the *Jean de France* intrigue was described to show its effect upon character; the *Busy Man* intrigue demonstrated Holberg's use of the aside to help maintain the audience's comprehension and acceptance of a complicated scheme. Therefore, only three intrigues will be examined in this chapter: one to expose a character's foible, one to unite young lovers, and one to perpetrate a swindle.

The Honourable Ambition demonstrates the intrigue designed to cure a character of his foible. Jeronimus, who wishes to improve his social standing, has begun by trying to act like an aristocrat. When he hears that a baron is visiting the area, he sends his servant, Arv, to invite the baron to dinner. Instead of bringing back the baron, Arv returns with Henrich, servant of Jeronimus's future son-in-law, Leander, disguised as a baron. At this point Henrich merely wants the fun of seeing how far the social-climbing Jeronimus will go in attempting to advance his position. Henrich praises Jeronimus for his social graces, which are actually crude and ridiculous. Enticed by Henrich, Jeronimus brags about what he has done to merit a higher social position. Finally, after demonstrating to the audience how ridiculous Jeronimus is when he attempts to act well-bred, Henrich promises him an advancement in social position.

Unfortunately, this "promise" causes Jeronimus to break off the engagement between his daughter and Leander on the grounds that Leander is now not good enough for his family. With this news, Henrich again returns as the baron, swindling Jeronimus out of one hundred ducats. Leander saves the day by revealing Henrich to be his own servant instead of a baron. Jeronimus, embarrassed, sees the folly of his ways and promises to abandon his social ambitions. Leander and Leonora again happily await their marriage, gratified to know that Jeronimus will no longer behave pompously.

It is evident that the characters' actions are based upon Jeronimus's desire for higher social status. The intrigue, the comic business resulting from Jeronimus's attempts to act well-bred, and the swindle all derive from the situation. Even though this particular intrigue involves a minor swindle, its main function is to expose the foible of social climbing.

The second most prominent use of the intrigue, to unite young lovers, is the major concern in *Pernille's Short Experience as a Lady*. An old man, Jeronimus, visits the Leonard family with the intent of arranging a marriage between his stepson, Leander, and their daughter, Leonora. However, when he learns that the sixteen-year-old virgin is both beautiful and wealthy, he decides to marry her himself. Jeronimus deceives Leonora's mother, Magdelone, into promising the girl to him. The young lovers are heartbroken. Leander's servant, Henrich, decides to invent a scheme that will unite them.

Just before Jeronimus arrives at the Leonard home for the wedding, Henrich arrives disguised as a monk, claiming that he has just heard an old woman's final confession. Lucie, the old woman, was the mother of Pernille, Leonora's maid, and was well known to the family. Lucie confessed to having switched her own daughter with Magdelone's daughter when they were babies; by doing so, she would give her own daughter the advantage of a good education and money, while Magdelone's daughter would be raised a servant. The story causes an uproar, but the Leonard family decides that Pernille is their rightful daughter and that she should have the birthright.

In comes Jeronimus, looking ridiculous because he has dressed himself in the most dashing of young styles. When he learns of the switch, and that Leonora, his intended, is really a servant, he claims that it is the daughter of Magdelone—not specifically Leonora—who is to be his wife. Instead of comprehending his true motive of gaining wealth, Magdelone believes him and gives her blessing to her future son-in-law, even though he is older than she. Unaware of his servant's scheme, Leander enters and hears the story. He declares that he does not care about social position and that he will marry Leonora even if she is a servant. So the marriages take place: Jeronimus to Pernille and Leander to Leonora.

With a knock at the door, Lucie enters, as alive as she can be. She had been instructed by Henrich to arrive at just this time. The story of switching the babies is revealed as false, and the "monk" is revealed as Leander's servant, Henrich. In the end, Pernille is happy because she has married a rich old man; she is now a lady and will inherit his fortune when he dies. Leander and Leonora are happy because they are truly in love. Magdelone and Leonard are happy because they now understand Jeronimus's true intentions and have escaped their consequences. Only Jeronimus is angry, because he is stuck with a wife who has no dowry or inheritance. Furthermore, it will cost him a fortune to outfit her as a lady in the social position to which she has just advanced.

In *The Honourable Ambition* and *Pernille's Short Experience as a Lady*, the intrigues, as well as the characters and comic business, result from the situation set up at the beginning of the play. Just as the situation provides a framework for the intrigues and comic business, the intrigues provide a framework for comedy through the use of disguise, misunderstanding, and victimization.

The third type of intrigue is designed to swindle a character rather than cure a foible or unite young lovers. For example, in *The Peasant Boy in Pawn*, the peasant boy is a country simpleton who unwittingly allows two city slickers to use him to perpetrate a hoax. They dress him up as a baron and pass him off as a rich man's stupid son. Unwary businessmen house them at an inn, wine them, dine them, and even give them jewels and expensive brocades to examine for possible purchase. When the businessmen return to the inn the next morning, the rascals have absconded with the goods, leaving the peasant boy asleep in his room. The businessmen confront the "baron" to receive payment for their jewels, brocade, horses, and entertainment, but discover that he is simply a dumb country boy who has no money, knows nothing of the hoax, and is too stupid to even realize what has happened. They are ready to hang him when his parents arrive. Realizing that the swindle was not the boy's fault, the businessmen release him to his parents on the grounds that they will never again allow the boy to come to the city alone.

Here again, the intrigue, even though used to bring about misfortune, is funny and enjoyable. The likable country rube gains the audience's sympathy because he is unaware of the mischief he is causing. Since the audience also knows that he will be left alone to take the blame, they are concerned about his welfare.

While all three of these examples demonstrate Holberg's ability to create a basic comic situation allowing for comic business, characters, and intrigues, they are similar in another way: all of them are in some way based upon a person who attempts to assume the social manners of a rank higher than his "proper" social standing. Hans Brix points out that this device was one of Holberg's most successful. He believes that Holberg's audience was very receptive to the idea and found such situations hilarious.[3] This supposition is supported by Holberg in epistle 72: "There is however one tendency in which the nation has persisted in this period of volatility—to wit, appetite for rank or the so-called *honnête ambition* [honourable ambition]. This seems more and more to be becoming the object of the Danes' attentive consideration."[4] This subject, the "appetite for rank," is the foundation for eight of the plays in which intrigues are an important plot device. These scripts include those cited above and *Jeppe of the Hill, Henrich and Pernille,* and *The Political Tinker.* In addition, numerous other Holberg comedies, such as *The Maternity Room* and *The Fortunate Shipwreck*, use this story idea as the basis for incidental comic business.

Comic Business

There are many types of comic business, or nonverbal aspects of comedy, in Holberg's plays, and like the intrigue, they are based upon the underlying comic situation in each play. While Holberg uses different business in each play depending upon the characters and actions, certain types of comic business recur no matter what the situations or the personalities: the disguise, physical humiliation of a main character, and stage fights and beatings.

Disguises are essential to the schemes in Holberg's intrigues, but they are also successfully used in other situations. For example, in *The Mascarade*, Henrich disguises himself as a ghost and "appears" to Arv, thus persuading him to confess to some of his more recent escapades; Henrich then uses that information to blackmail him. Later in the same play, Henrich disguises himself as a Jewish rabbi in order to sneak a message past Jeronimus to Leonora, resulting in some funny business when Jeronimus and Leonora arrive at the scene at the same time. Henrich attempts to reveal himself to Leonora without betraying his disguise to Jeronimus. Finally, Arv enters, recognizes Henrich, and is able to reverse the earlier blackmail situation by threatening to reveal Henrich's true identity.

One of the most humorous disguise situations is

found in *Without Head or Tail*. Henrich finds a devil's costume in the street and puts it on; just then a rival servant, Haagen, comes along and really believes Henrich to be the devil. Henrich decides to have fun playing along:

HENRICH (*Aside.*) I'll scare him more than he's ever been in his life! (*To Haagen.*) You evil rogue! Your time has come!

HAAGEN Oh, Lucifer! Don't hurt me!

HENRICH (*Roars with laughter.*)

HAAGEN Your excellency! Spare my life and give me time to repent.

HENRICH You must come with me unless you immediately confess your sins.

HAAGEN The day before yesterday I stole four rixdaler from my master. When he questioned me about it I vowed that I hadn't done it. A week ago I was supposed to buy my master a pound of tobacco, but I only bought a half a pound. To fill it in I put a half a pound of pebbles in the sack. And last night I went to bed with a girl named Nille.

HENRICH Which girl is that?

HAAGEN She's engaged to my master's servant, Henrich.

HENRICH Have you done it before?

HAAGEN Seven or eight times.

HENRICH Did she allow you to pay for it?

HAAGEN No. She pays me. Last night she gave me this rare two-mark coin that her fiancé had given her.

HENRICH (*Bellows and chases Haagen away.*) [act II, scene 6]

Henrich's use of the disguise in this scene results in one of the funniest incidents in the play. It is funny first of all because the audience knows who the "devil" is, but Haagen does not; then, when the tables are turned on Henrich by Haagen's confession to making love with Henrich's fiancée, even more laughter is elicited. Holberg's use of the disguise in his plays greatly adds to the comedy and the audience's enjoyment.

Another type of comic business Holberg often uses is the physical humiliation of the main character by adding insult to injury. For example, in *Jean de France*, just before Jean returns to Paris, a creditor takes his watch, wig, and clothes in payment for a gambling debt. A similar, but even greater insult occurs in *Ulysses von Ithacia*. Ulysses has returned home from his forty-year war, only to learn that he has lost his kingdom and his wife. Penniless and unknown in his own country, he is sitting on a rock, rejected by all, when two Jews appear:

ULYSSES I must sit and await the return of my true servant.
(*Two Jews enter.*)
FIRST JEW That's the trouble with renting clothes to those acting troupes. They take the clothes and we don't get paid for a whole week.
SECOND JEW Isn't that the truth, Ephraim! We just never learn. Look over there. Isn't that man sitting in the dirt wearing *our* clothes? (*Goes over and jerks Ulysses' arm.*) Hey! What do you mean sleeping around in our clothes?
ULYSSES Who would dare to wake the great Ulysses?
FIRST JEW It's me. Remember? Me, Ephraim!
ULYSSES I do not know thee. Thou appearest to be a wanderer.
SECOND JEW All of Israel's children are wanderers.
ULYSSES Tell me, Noble Wanderer, what is the situation in Ithacia?
SECOND JEW I don't have the time for that now. I've got to get those clothes ready for tonight's masked ball.
ULYSSES How dare thee lay a hand upon my noble body? Remove thyself from me or thou shalt feel the effect of my great wrath!

SECOND JEW Give me the clothes or you'll feel the effect of our
    country's laws!
ULYSSES Is this my reward for forty years of fighting?
(*The Jews remove his clothes.*)
FIRST JEW If you've been away for forty years, you have to pay
    forty years' rent. We have to make a living, you know.
ULYSSES Oh heavens! I wish that I had remained at home and
    destroyed all of the Jews instead of going to Troy! Then
    my reign would not have ended so abruptly!
                                                    [act V, scene 5]

This scene is funny for several reasons: first, the
treatment of the general as a common man; second, the
introduction of two Jews into a tale about ancient Greece;
third, the fact that the Jews have current Copenhagen attitudes and occupations; and finally, the Jews' disrobing
of the once-great Ulysses merely so they can re-rent his
forty-year-old clothes for that night's masked ball. (Holberg's use of anachronisms, by the way, is peculiar to this
play.) Another dimension of the humor is not explicit in
the script: the German acting troupes apparently did rent
their costumes, and the Jewish lessors did have trouble
collecting for their use. So the "forty years" line takes on
new meaning in this context, and the joke becomes a
final satirical dig at the lack of time consistencies in the
German sagas.

Holberg also makes good use of stage fights and beatings as comic business. There is hardly a play which does
not include someone getting "boxed on the ears." In this
typical stage fight from *The Peasant Boy in Pawn*, two
innkeepers are arguing over which one of them will
house the visiting "baron":

FIRST INNKEEPER What did you say?

SECOND INNKEEPER I said the accommodations are lousy in your inn!

LEERBEUTEL Gentlemen! Please stop your arguing.

SECOND INNKEEPER It's just as I've been saying, my lord. If you take your lodging at my inn, you'll have better service and you'll be away from the disturbances here.

FIRST INNKEEPER Anyone who says my service is inferior is a snake!

SECOND INNKEEPER Well, I say that you're a bread thief and that you'd steal the food off a blind man's plate!

FIRST INNKEEPER If anyone is a bread thief, it's you!

(They fight, grabbing each other by the hair. Finally, Leerbeutel is able to separate them and drive away the Second Innkeeper.)   [act II, scene 2]

Sometimes the fights in Holberg's plays provide laughs, as in the beating Jeppe gets from his wife in *Jeppe of the Hill*; on other occasions, such as the one cited above, they provide good stage action and excitement.

Finally, Holberg not only wrote comic business into the scripts, he continued to add comic business after the plays were performed. Much of this business is not written down in the scripts, although it is always included in the Holberg productions at the Royal Danish Theatre; it is said to have been invented by Holberg during the earliest Grønnegade productions in order to make various scenes more entertaining. For instance, during Jeppe's first monologue, it is traditional that he dress himself as he speaks. In the second act of *The Political Tinker*, when Herman is preparing his house for the "political college," it is traditional that Herman and Henrich set the table while they speak. As they work, a dish of food is dropped. Henrich finally becomes angry and pushes it into Herman's face.[5] Some traditional comic business is recorded in notes prefacing the comedies; other business is merely passed down from one generation of actors to the next.

Just as the basic comic situation in a play provides the foundation for comic characters, dialogue, and intrigues, it also provides the foundation for other comic business. While there is business unique to each play, such as the traditional business, several comic devices appear again and again: Holberg used disguises, fights, and the ability to add insult to injury through comic activities consistently to provoke laughter. But the basic situations not only provide the groundwork for comic devices, they occasionally provide for music, dance, and spectacle as well.

Other Stage Activity: Music, Dance, and Spectacle

From the beginning of theatre in ancient Greece, music, dance, and spectacle have played an important part in the drama. Holberg also found place, limited though it might be, for these dimensions of entertainment. Music and dance are seldom an actual part of the comedies, except in unusual cases as a comic device (as Jean de France's dancing in the street is a demonstration of his foible). Instead, music and dance are usually used between scenes or acts for their pure and unintegrated entertainment value. A typical instance occurs in act II, scene 8 of *The Peasant Boy in Pawn* when the "baron" and his guests go into the inn for dinner. Holberg's stage directions call for "musicians to play select numbers while a dancer performs a beautiful dance."

Sometimes a musical interlude can perform a more important role. For example, the only love scene in any Holberg comedy is depicted by a musical interlude. The stage directions between acts I and II of *The Mascarade* specify: "The masked ball is presented. Leander falls in love with a masked woman, who is Leonora. They unmask and exchange rings. After fifteen minutes the curtain falls."

Thus, Holberg's use of music and dance, though occasional, provides additional entertainment in some of his comedies. Music and dance usually are not totally integrated into the action, but instead serve to provide variety. They were first added to Holberg's comedies after it became the policy of the Grønnegade Theatre to show shorter plays and to have a greater variety and quantity of additional amusements between acts.

Holberg uses spectacle in a similar manner. In this example from act IV, scene 8 of *Witchcraft*, spectacle is at least partially integrated into the story: "A drummer enters and circles the theatre three times. One by one a crowd gathers around him, especially children and old women. Then he reads his proclamation about the witches. After reading it, he again beats his drum and exits, followed by the group, who make a great amount of noise."

In *Plutus*, another lengthy procession circles the theatre three times. The pompous display is to welcome the god of wealth, Plutus, to the poor country where the action takes place. After exploiting the pomp for its theatri-

cal value, Holberg turns the procession into a device for
Diogenes to express his contempt of the advent of Plutus:

*(A procession enters playing music. It circles the theatre three
times. At the end of each circle, it stops and the people shout,
"Vivat Plutus!" Then a drum and trumpet fanfare sounds.
When the third round is completed, three dancers dance an
artful dance. Diogenes acts as though he is sitting in an inn,
grimacing. After a while he grabs a cane and chases the people
away as they scream and make noise.)*

DIOGENES Go ahead! Just try to make music, you scab-throats!
Soon this country will resemble the tragedies that close
the performances at the comedy house. Hah! I'll dance for
you! I'll dance so you understand the tragedy to come!

*(He dances a very bizarre dance with his wooden shoes. The
tune, played either on bagpipes or lyre, is sorrowful. Plutus
suddenly enters. The music stops, but Diogenes continues to
dance.)*   [act II, scenes 5 & 6]

Thus, Holberg not only invented funny situations
and business, but also added music, dance, and spectacle
to some of his comedies for their theatrical qualitites
after it became the custom to show a shorter play with
various other entertainments. However, it is Holberg's
ability to invent comic situations and then build upon
them with other aspects of comedy that has enabled his
plays to retain their popularity. Had the humor of the
plays been merely topical, it would now be lost to many
of its audiences because of political and social changes.
But since most of Holberg's comic devices are based upon
universally comic situations, they remain potent.

An examination of the unsuccessful Holberg comedies verifies this hypothesis. The five least successful

comedies, in terms of number of performances at the Royal Danish Theatre, are the five-act version of *Gert Westphaler, The Burial of Danish Comedy, The Republic, A Philosopher in His Own Estimation,* and *Sganarel's Travels to the Philosophical Land.*

Three of these comedies—*The Republic, A Philosopher in His Own Estimation,* and *Sganarel's Travels*—deal with some aspect of Holberg's personal philosophy. Interestingly, they were all among the plays Holberg wrote during the 1750s after the reopening of the Danish theatres. *The Republic,* Holberg's most abstract comedy, informs the government that it is failing by trying too hard to please everyone. The two "Philosopher" plays describe aspects of Holberg's beliefs about philosophy and what kind of person a true philosopher should be. All three of these comedies are personal and lack the important universal elements present in the most popular comedies.

The Burial of Danish Comedy was written for one specific occasion, the closing of the Danish theatres in 1727. That is the only time the play was performed. Apparently yesterday's news was old news even in the eighteenth century.

Finally, the five-act version of *Gert Westphaler* was unsuccessful. True, the foible it satirizes—overtalkativeness—is universal, and the situation of a man talking himself out of his forthcoming marriage, his job, and his social position is humorous. But the fault being ridiculed also proved to be the downfall of the play. Gert Westphaler simply talks too much. The audience (as well as the characters in the play) gets tired of listening to Gert ramble on and on about the same boring topics. Holberg's revised one-act version, omitting much of the actual talking, has been very successful in the theatre.

Holberg's situations, like his characters, are mostly stock. They resemble in type, and often in specifics, the comic situations which have been successful from ancient Greece until today. But for the most part, Holberg was able to adapt them to his own comedies in a masterful way, as the foundation for his other comic devices.

SEVEN

Conclusion

IN THE EARLY SUMMER of 1722, when René Montaigu came to Ludvig Holberg requesting him to write original Danish plays for the new Danish language theatre, Holberg was ripe for the idea. He had already begun a campaign—so far unsuccessful—to prepare Denmark to accept the new literary forms and philosophies current throughout the rest of Europe. He had published his *Introduction to the History of the Principal Kingdoms of Europe* and his first philosophical work, *Introduction to the Science of Natural Law and the Law of Nations*—both in Danish, a language that Danish scholars thought incapable of expressing important thoughts. In addition, Holberg had written his four-part epic satire, *Peder Paars*, which had been popular with the public, but not with the academicians whom he wished to influence. Having failed to gain scholarly acceptance of new literary forms or use of the vernacular, Holberg decided to write plays for the middle-class citizens of Copenhagen. His comedies were an immediate popular success, and they have retained this popularity for over two hundred and fifty years.

Even though Holberg arrived at his method of writing plays through the experience provided by a university education, travel, and a deep interest in history and philosophy, he wrote plays which succeed for the same reasons as Molière's or Neil Simon's: comic situations, business, characters, and dialogue. Because his humor springs from the situations and characters, his jokes and comic business remain as funny today as they were in the eighteenth century. Holberg's comic genius, operating through universal, middle-class characters, accounts for his popularity in the theatre through the years.

Some techniques have potency in the theatre at any time, in any place. Holberg's success stems from his ability to sense and use these techniques superbly, with timeless appeal. However, it would be a mistake to conclude that Holberg was ordinary because he used common and popular dramatic techniques. Rather, it is the extraordinary writer who is so in tune with the common taste that he or she can recreate life on the stage in such a convincing and triumphant way.

Ludvig Holberg's plays are similar to the plays of Shakespeare in the sense that the majority of them have remained popular.[1] For example, there have been more Holberg performances at the Royal Danish Theatre than any other playwright's. A comparison made in 1966 found that Holberg's comedies had been performed 4,167 times; J. L. Heiberg's plays, 3,033 times; Christian Hostrup's plays, 1,417 times.[2] However, when the number of performances of specific plays is examined, the tally is quite different. Heiberg's *Elf Hill* enjoyed the most performances, playing 911 times. His *No* and *The Critic and the Animal* played 372 and 371 times respectively. Hostrup's musical comedy, *Adventure on Foot*, had 418 performances. During the same period of time, Holberg's *Jeppe of the Hill* and *Henrich and Pernille*, his most frequently performed plays, had only 354 performances each.[3] Thus, while the plays of other playwrights have had fewer total performances, individual plays by these other writers have been performed more often than any single Holberg play. Holberg's success has not been sustained by repeated performances of any small group of plays, but by the rotation of a majority of his thirty-three comedies. Since the beginning of the Royal Danish Theatre in 1748, twenty-two of Holberg's comedies have been consistently successful. The following table lists the comedies in the order of their total number of performances as of the 1979–80 season of the Royal Danish Theatre; it also compares the number of performances as of 1922 and the number of performances since then.

Table 1
Holberg's Comedies in Rank Order of Their Number
of Performances at the Royal Danish Theatre

	Performances		
Play	*as of 1922*	*since 1922*	*Total as of 31 May 1980*
Big Hits:			
Erasmus Montanus	216	167	383
The Busy Man	221	146	367
Jeppe of the Hill	234	120	354
Henrich and Pernille	190	164	354
The Political Tinker	250	103	353
The Mascarade	199	102	301
The Maternity Room	184	116	300

Table 1 (continued)

Play	Performances		
	as of 1922	since 1922	Total as of 31 May 1980
Hits:			
The Invisible Ladies	118	99	217
The Christmas Room	113	102	215
The Fortunate Shipwreck	84	116	200
Jean de France	96	101	197
The Fickle Woman	102	64	166
Gert Westphaler (one-act)	152	0	152
Jacob von Tyboe	146	0	146
Pernille's Short Experience as a Lady	136	0	136
Witchcraft	70	35	105
Successful:			
Diderich—Terror of Mankind	85	0	85
The Honourable Ambition	80	3	83
The Peasant Boy in Pawn	77	0	77
Ulysses von Ithacia	70	0	70
The Eleventh of June	59	3	62
Don Ranudo	43	14	57
Limited Success:			
Plutus	47	0	47
Journey to the Spring	43	4	47
Abracadabra	42	0	42
The Bridegroom's Metamorphosis	36	0	36
Melampe	36	0	36
Unsuccessful:			
The Arabian Powder	19	0	19
Without Head or Tail	9	0	9
Sganarel's Travels	6	0	6
A Philosopher in His Own Estimation	5	0	5
The Republic	2	0	2
Gert Westphaler (five-act)	0	0	0
The Burial of Danish Comedy	0	0	0

The most recent Holberg productions in the Royal Danish Theatre's repertory were *The Fortunate Shipwreck* (1974–76), *Jean de France* (1976–78), *The Invisible Ladies* and *The Christmas Room* (1978–79), and *Ulysses von Ithacia* (1980–81).

These production statistics further substantiate that those comedies with universal characters and situations have been most successful. A few of the comedies enjoyed limited success when they were first written, but have since lost their popularity. Apparently the situation or the ridiculed foibles in those plays are not universal enough to sustain interest. The least successful comedies have been those written to support Holberg's personal opinions regarding philosophy and government. The majority of the plays with lasting appeal are the earliest comedies. As time passed, Holberg seemed less and less able to choose universally comic characters or situations. Indeed, in his final six comedies, he seems to have lost his ability to portray the universality of human nature.

The dramaturgy of Holberg's comedies indicates that they should be translated into English. Given the thoughtful artistic preparations that go into any production of a period script, Holberg's comedies could be as successful in English-speaking countries as in Scandinavia and Northern Europe.

Notes
Bibliography
Index

Notes

One

1. Edvard Brandes, *Holberg og Hans Scene* (Copenhagen: Gyldendal, 1898), pp. 17–25.
2. For more complete biographical information see *Ludvig Holberg* by F. J. Billeskov Jansen (New York: Twayne Publishers, Inc., 1974) or *Danske Litteratur Historie*, vol. 1, *Fra Runerne til Johannes Ewald*, by Gustav Albeck and F. J. Billeskov Jansen (Copenhagen: Politikens Forlag, 1967).
3. For more detailed information see *Den Danske Skueplads Paa Holbergs Tid* by Alfred Jeppesen (Copenhagen: Martins Forlag, 1972).
4. Holberg, quoted by Francis Bull in the *Holberg Aarbog* (1920), pp. 38–39.
5. Holberg, quoted in *Den Danske Skueplads Paa Holbergs Tid*, p. 39.
6. Molière, "A Doctor in Spite of Himself", in *The Misanthrope and Other Plays*, trans. by John Wood (Baltimore: Penguin Books, 1968), p. 187.
7. Translated by Oscar J. Campbell in *Comedies of Holberg* (1914; reprint, New York: Benjamin Blom, 1968), p. 151.

8. Holberg, quoted by Carl S. Petersen and Vilhelm Andersen, *Illustreret Dansk Litteraturhistorie*, vol. 2, (Copenhagen: Gyldendal, 1934), p. 62.

9. Holberg, trans. by Campbell in *Comedies of Holberg*, pp. 243–44. For this section on influences I am indebted to Campbell's book, which provides a comprehensive examination of the literary sources of Holberg's comedies.

10. Holberg, trans. by Campbell in *Comedies of Holberg*, pp. 250–51.

11. Ben Jonson, "Introduction to *Every Man Out of His Humour*," in *Dramatic Theory and Criticism*, ed. by Bernard F. Dukore (New York: Holt, Rinehart and Winston, Inc., 1974), p. 186.

12. Campbell, *Comedies of Holberg*, p. 252.

13. Holberg, *Selected Essays of Ludvig Holberg*, trans. by P. M. Mitchell (Lawrence, Kans.: University of Kansas Press, 1955), pp. 106–7.

14. Holberg, trans. by Campbell in *Comedies of Holberg*, p. 313.

Two

1. Petersen and Andersen, *Illustreret Dansk Litteraturhistorie*, pp. 45–52.

2. P. Hansen, *Den Danske Skueplads*, vol. 1 (Copenhagen, 1889), p. 118.

3. Hans Brix, "En Aften Paa Komedie," *Tilskueren* (1922), p. 161.

4. Quoted by Billeskov Jansen in *Dansk Litteratur Historie*, vol. 1. (Copenhagen: Politikens Forlag, 1967), pp. 290–91.

5. P. F. Suhms, *Samtale imellem Hans og Peer*, vol. 1 of *Suhms Samlede Skrifter* (Copenhagen, 1788), pp. 51–64.

6. The quotes in this section from Holberg's essays were translated by P. M. Mitchell in *Selected Essays of Ludvig Holberg*. See pp. 56–58, 75, 95–98.

7. There is no fifth scene in the second act. The actual line in act II, scene 2 reads, "They can debate about whether I died on land or sea." While there is something of a pun in the Danish *"lands eller vands,"* ("land or sea"), the wit for which Holberg is being chided lies in the fact that Jeppe is apparently ridiculing the polemical debates that scholars had on such issues. However, it does seem likely that Jeppe would know of these. After all, Holberg's audience would not have liked *Peder Paars* had they not known of such debates. So rather than being a "witty" remark, it might be an observation totally within the realm of Jeppe's knowledge.

8. Brandes, *Holberg og Hans Scene*, p. 36.

9. Jørgen Stegelmann, *Hvem er Hvem hos Holberg: En Holberg Håndbog* (Copenhagen: Thaning & Appel, 1974), pp. 251–52.

10. Hans Brix, *Ludvig Holbergs Komedier* (Copenhagen: Gyldendal, 1942).

Three

1. Jeppesen, *Den Danske Skueplads Paa Holbergs Tid*, pp. 34–35. Also refer to Vilh. Møller, "Omkring Grønnegade Teatret," *Tilskueren* (1898): 650–62.

2. J. C. Normann, *Holberg Paa Teatret* (Copenhagen: Gyldendalske Boghandel, 1909), p. 2.

3. Jeppesen, *Den Danske Skueplads Paa Holbergs Tid*, pp. 35–36.

4. Ibid., p. 59.

5. Ibid., p. 153.

Four

1. Holberg, *Selected Essays*, trans. by P. M. Mitchell, p. 62.

2. Translated by Campbell, *Comedies of Holberg*, pp. 317–18.

Six

1. J. W. Lange, "How Plautus and Shakespeare Make Us Laugh," *Classical Bulletin* 9 (1932/33): 41.
2. Ibid., pp. 41–43.
3. Hans Brix, "En Aften Paa Komedie," p. 162.
4. Holberg, *Selected Essays*, trans. by P. M. Mitchell, p. 62.
5. Normann, *Holberg Paa Teatret*, pp. 9–10.

Seven

1. Unlike the professional American theatre where a successful play may have a single run well over one thousand performances, the nature of the Danish theatre's repertory system generates great numbers of performances very gradually. For example, the major triumph of the first sixty years (1748–1808) of the Royal Danish Theatre was *Jeppe of the Hill*. It was considered an active play in the theatre's repertoire all sixty seasons, but was actually performed only ninety-nine times. This is the result of performing for the theatre audience of a country whose population is comparatively small.
2. Alf Henriques, *The Royal Theatre Past and Present* (Copenhagen Office, 1967), p. 38.
3. Ibid., pp. 38–40.

Bibliography

PRIMARY SOURCES

Readings in English

Ludvig Holberg's Comedies

Comedies (*Jeppe of the Hill, The Political Tinker, Erasmus Montanus*). Translated by O. J. Campbell and Frederic Schenck. Vol. 1 of *Scandinavian Classics*. New York: American Scandinavian Foundation, 1915.

Four Plays By Holberg (*The Fussy Man, The Masked Ladies, The Weathercock, Masquerades*). Translated by Henry Alexander. Princeton, N.J.: Princeton University Press, 1946.

Seven One-Act Plays by Holberg (*The Talkative Barber, The Arabian Powder, The Christmas Party, Diderich the Terrible, The Peasant in Pawn, Sganarel's Journey to the Land of the Philosopher, The Changed Bridegroom*). Translated by Henry Alexander. Princeton, N.J.: Princeton University Press, 1950.

Three Comedies (*Henry and Pernilla, Captain Bombastes*

Thunderton, Scatterbrains). Translated by Lieut. Colonel
H. W. L. Hime. London: Longmans and Company, 1912.
*Three Comedies (The Transformed Peasant, The Arabian Pow-
der, The Healing Spring).* Translated by Reginald Spink.
London: Heinemann, 1957.

Other Writings by Ludvig Holberg

*Ludvig Holberg: Memoirs. An Eighteenth-Century Danish
Contribution to International Understanding.* Edited by
Stewart E. Frazer. Leiden, Holland: E. J. Brill, 1970.
Journey of Niels Klim to the World Underground. Introduced
and edited by James I. McNab, Jr. Lincoln, Neb.: Univer-
sity of Nebraska Press, 1960.
Journey to the World Underground. Edited by Michael F. Shu-
grue. New York: Garland, 1974.
Peder Paars. Translated by Bergliot Stromsoe. Lincoln, Neb.:
University of Nebraska Press and American-Scandinavian
Foundation, 1962.
Selected Essays of Ludvig Holberg. Translated by P. M.
Mitchell. Lawrence, Kans.: University of Kansas Press,
1955.

Readings in Danish

Major Danish Editions of Ludvig Holberg's Works

Festudgaven. 6 vols. Copenhagen: H. Aschehoug and Company, 1922:
    Comoedier og De Populære Skrifter. Vols. 1–3. Edited by
    Carl Roos et al.
    Epistler og Småstykker i Udvalg. Edited by Francis Bull.
    Niels Klim og Levnetsbrevene. Edited by S. P. Thomas and
    A. H. Winsnes.

Peder Paars og Skæmtedigtene. Edited by Georg Christensen.

Holbergs Samlede Skrifter. Copenhagen: Carl S. Petersen et al., 1913–63

Mindre Poetisk Skrifter. Copenhagen: H. Aschehoug and Company, 1922.

Værker i Tolv Bind. Edited by F. J. Billeskov Jansen. Copenhagen: Gyldendal, 1969–71.

SECONDARY SOURCES

Works Cited

Albeck, Gustav, and Billeskov Jansen, F. J. *Fra Runerne til Johannes Ewald.* Vol. 1 of *Dansk Litteratur Historie.* Copenhagen: Politikens Forlag, 1967.

Billeskov Jansen, F. J. *Ludvig Holberg.* Translated by David Stoner. New York: Twayne Publishers, Inc., 1974.

Brandes, Edvard. *Holberg og Hans Scene.* Copenhagen: Gyldendal, 1898.

Brix, Hans. "En Aften Paa Komedie." *Tilskueren* (1922): 159–64.

———. *Ludvig Holbergs Komedier.* Copenhagen: Gyldendalske Boghandel, Nordisk Forlag, 1942.

Bull, Francis. "Om Holbergs Femten Første Komedier." *Holberg Aarbog.* Edited by Francis Bull and Carl S. Petersen. 1(1920): 36–67.

Campbell, Jr., Oscar J. *The Comedies of Holberg.* 1914. Reprint. New York: Benjamin Blom, 1968.

Dukore, Bernard F., ed. *Dramatic Theory and Criticism.* New York: Holt, Rinehart, and Winston, Inc., 1974.

Hansen, P. *Den Danske Skueplads.* Vol. 1. Copenhagen, 1889.

Henriques, Alf. *The Royal Theatre Past and Present.* Copenhagen: Krohns Office, 1967.

Jeppesen, Alfred. *Den Danske Skueplads Paa Holbergs Tid.* Copenhagen: Martins Forlag, 1972.

Lange, J. W. "How Plautus and Shakespeare Make Us Laugh." *Classical Bulletin* 9 (1932/33).

Molière. *The Misanthrope and Other Plays.* Translated by John Wood. Baltimore: Penguin Books, 1960.

Møller, Vilh. "Omkring Grønnegade-Teatret." *Tilskueren* (1898): 650–62.

Normann, J. C. *Holberg Paa Teatret.* Copenhagen: Gyldendalske Boghandel, 1909.

Petersen, Carl S., and Andersen, Vilhelm. *Illustreret Dansk Litteraturhistorie.* Vol. 2. Copenhagen: Gyldendal, 1934.

Rosenstand-Goiske, Peder. *Den Dramatiske Journal.* 3 vols. Edited by Carl Behrens. Copenhagen: H. H. Thieles Bogtrykkeri, 1915.

Stegelmann, Jørgen. *Hvem er Hvem hos Holberg: En Holberg Haåndbog.* Copenhagen: Thaning & Appel, 1974.

Suhms, P. F. *Samtale imellem Hans og Peer.* Vol. 1 of *Suhms Samlede Skrifter.* Copenhagen, 1788.

Supplementary Sources

The following bibliography is provided to foster and aid continued research in Ludvig Holberg's dramatic writings.

Andersen, Vilhelm. *Holberg Billedbog.* Copenhagen: H. Aschehoug and Company, 1922.

———. "Holberg's Henrich." *Tilskueren* (1906): 56–74, 132–42.

———. *Litteratur billeder.* 2 vols. Copenhagen, 1905–7.

———. *Ludvig Holberg Paa Tersløsegaard.* Copenhagen, 1904.

———. "Ophaven til Holbergs Komedier." *Sprog og Litteratur* (Copenhagen 1914).

Anthology of Danish Literature. Bilingual edition. Edited by F. J. Billeskov Jansen and P. M. Mitchell. Carbondale, Ill.: Southern Illinois University Press, 1964. (Paperback: *Anthology of Danish Literature: Middle Ages to Romanticism.* Arcturus Books, 1971.

Argetsinger, Gerald S. "The Dramaturgy of Ludvig Holberg's Comedies." Diss.: Bowling Green State University, 1975.

Atlung, Knud. *Det Kongelige Teater 1889–1939: En Statistisk Fremstilling.* Copenhagen, 1942.

Aumont, Arthur. "Den Danske Skueplads for 150 Aar Siden." *Politiken,* 18 December 1898.

———. "Holberg-Traditionen paa den danske Skueplads." *Tilskueren* (1887): 631–40.

———. , and Collin, Edgar. *Det Danske Nationalteater 1748–1889: En Statistik Fremstilling af Det Kongelig Teaters Historie fra Skuepladsens Aabning Paa Kongens Nytorv.* 5 vols. Copenhagen 1896–1900.

Bang, Herman. "Holbergforestillingerne." *Tilskueren* (1885): 106–11.

Bay, Rud. "Et Besøg hos Jeronimus og Magdelone." *Fremtidens Nytaarsgave,* Ny R. II. (Copenhagen, 1883): 47–81.

———. "Konturer af Holbergs Tidsalder." *Fremtidens Nytaarsgavl,* Ny R. III. (Copenhagen, 1884): 144–67.

Billeskov Jansen, F. J. "Ludvig Holberg and Some French Thinkers." *Scandinavian Studies: Essays Presented to Dr. Henry Goddard Leach.* Seattle, 1965.

Bing, Just. "Den Holbergske Komedie." *Nordisk Tidsskrift* (1901): 493–515.

———. "Holbergs Første Livnetsbrev." *Danske Studier* (1904).

———. "Holbergs Livsanskuelse og Personlighed." *Danske Studier* (1905).

———. "Holberg, Rostgaard, og Montaigu." *Nordisk Tidsskrift* (1903).

Boye, A. E. "Fragmenter Over Holberg." Eight essays. *Athene, et Maanedskrift* 5, 8, 9(1815–17).

————. "Holberg i Tyskland." *Nyt Aftenblad*, no. 211 (1844).

Brandes, Georg. *Ludvig Holberg*. 1884. Reprint. Copenhagen: Gyldendals Uglebøger, 1969.

————. "Ludvig Holberg som Komedieforfatter." *Bilag til Ludvig Holbergs Comoedier*. Jubeludgaven. Copenhagen: Ernst Bojesens Kunst-Forlag, 1888. Pp. 5–42.

Brasch, Chr. H. *Om Robert Molesworths Skrift—"An Account of Denmark as It Was in the Year 1692."* Copenhagen, 1879.

Brix, Hans. "The Earliest Impressions of Holberg's Comedies." *Acta Philogica Scandinavica* 1(1926/27): 24–53.

————. "Et Par Bemærkninger til Holbergs Komedier." *Danske Studier* (1912): 131.

————. "Holberg og Teatre Italien." *Edda* 11(1919): 120–45.

————. "Holbergs Skueplads." *Tilskueren* 2(1919): 233–39.

————. "Om Kilderne til Holbergs Fem Første Komedier." *Tilskueren* (1922): 165–81.

————. "Om Tiden for Komediernes Tilblivelse." *Tilskueren* 2(1920): 113–20.

————. "Tekstkritiske Bemærkninger til Fem og Tyve af Holbergs Komedier." *Edda* 6(1916): 312–55.

————. "Til Arbejdsmetoden i Komedierne." *Holberg Aarbog*. Edited by Francis Bull and Carl S. Petersen. 3(1922): 84–106.

Bruun, Chr. "Et Par Ord om Baron Holberg." *Danske Tidsskrift* (1905).

————. "Nye Bidrag til Oplysning om den Danske Skueplads i dens Første Aar." *Danske Samlinger* 3(1868).

————. *Om Ludvig Holbergs Trende Epistler til en Højfornem Herre, Indholdende Hans Autobiografi*. Copenhagen, 1895.

Christensen, Nils. "Noko um Namna i Komediane til Holberg." *Syn og Segn* 35(Oslo, 1929).

Coyet, G. V. "Bemærkninger om Komedierne." *Edda* 29(1929): 107–9.

Daae, L. "Optegnelser til Ludvig Holbergs Biografi." *Historisk Tidsskrift*, 1st series, 2(1872).

Dahlerup, Verner. "Om Holbergs Sidste Autobiografi Epistle Nr. 447." *Historisk Tidsskrift*, 6th series, 4(1893).

de Jessen, F. "Louis Baron de Holberg, l'emule scandinave de Molière." *Revue de cours et conferences* 10(Paris, 1922).

Den Danske Skueplads. Copenhagen: Berlingske Forlag, 1943.

Dyrlund, F. "En Foregiven Gudsøn af Holberg." *Dania* 9(1902).

Eaton, J. W. "Holberg and Germany." *Journal of English and German Philosophy* 36(October 1937): 505–14.

Enrencron-Müller, H. *Forfatterlexikon Omfattende Danmark, Norge, og Island*. Vol. 2. Copenhagen: H. Aschehoug and Company, 1934.

Friis, Oluf. "Holberg og den Danske Skueplads." *Letterst. tidskrift* (1922): 435–44.

Hagelberg, Nina. "Et Par af Holbergs Leonoraer." *Vor Ungdom* (1901): 581–93.

Hansen, P. *Illustreret Dansk Litteratur Historie*. 2nd ed. 2 vols. Copenhagen, 1889–96.

Helland, Amund. "Citater fra Holberg's Komedier og Peder Paars." *Festskrift til W. Nyegaard* (Oslo, 1913): 32–47.

Hennings, A. A. F. "Komedierne var vel kendt af Bønderne." *Arkiv og Museum* 1(1899): 183.

Henriques, Alf; Krogh, Torben; and Hellsen, Henry. *Teatret Paa Kongens Nytorv, 1748–1948*. Copenhagen, 1948.

Hoffory, Jul. "Om Holbergs Komediedigtning." *Tilskueren* (1887): 423–38.

"Holberg og Hans Scene." *Nationaltidende*, no. 8434–35 (1899).

Holm, E. *Holbergs Statsretslige og Politiske Synsmaader*. Copenhagen, 1879.

Holm-Hansen, Henrik, ed. *Holberg Læst og Påskrevet*. Copenhagen: Royal Theatre, 1972.

Humbert, C. "Molière und Holberg." *Neue Jahrbücher für Philologie und Pädagogik* 124(1881): 376–90.

Hviid, A. C. *Udtog af en Dagbog Holden i Aarene 1770–80.* Copenhagen, 1787.

"Hvorledes de Holbergske Lystspil Kunde og Burde Gives Paa Skuepladsen." *Nyeste Skilderie af København* 25(1816): 17 and 26(1816): 60–61.

Høyberg, Wille. *Kjöbenhavnske Samlinger af Rare Trykte og Utrykte Piecer.* Copenhagen, 1754.

Jansen, F. J. Billeskov. See Billeskov Jansen, F. J.

Jensen, Bernhard. "Jeronimus." *Holberg Aarbog.* Edited by Francis Bull and Carl S. Petersen. 4(1923).

Josephson, Ludvig. "Skola vi Spela Holberg?" *Studier och Kritiker* 4 haft. 1(Stockholm, 1896).

Kahle, B. "Ludvig Holberg." *Neue Heidelberger Jahrbücher* 13.

Kall-Rasmussen, M. N. R. "Bidrag til L. Holbergs Biografi for Aarene 1702–14." *Historisk Tidsskrift*, 3rd series, 1(1858).

Kragh-Jacobsen, Svend. *Teaterårbogen, 1955–56.* Copenhagen, 1956.

———, and Christensen, Kaj. *25 Teatersæsoner: Københavnske Teater i Billeder og Repertoire, 1931–1956.* Copenhagen, 1956.

Krogh, Torben. *Holberg i Det Kongelig Teaters Ældste Regieprotokoller.* Copenhagen, 1943.

———. *Musik og Teater.* Copenhagen, 1955.

———. "Nye Teaterhistoriske Holbergfund." *Tilskueren* 2(1931): 81–100.

———. *Studier Over de Sceniske Opførelser af Holbergs Komedier i de Første Aar Paa Den Genoprettede Dansk Skueplads.* Copenhagen: St. f. s. o. O., 1929.

———. *Ældre Dansk Teater.* Copenhagen, 1940.

Kruuse, Jens. *Holbergs Maske.* Copenhagen: Gyldendal, 1964.

Langberg, Harald. *Kongens Teater—Komediehuset På Kongens Nytorv 1748–1744.* Copenhagen: Gyldendal, 1974.

Lauring, Palle. *Ej Blot Til Lyst—Det Kongelige Teater 1874–1974.* Copenhagen: Forum, 1974.

Legrelle, Arsene. *Holberg consideré comme imitateur de Molière.* Thesis, University of Paris, 1864.

Lenning, Hjalmar. "Holbergkomedierna och Danmark's National-Teater." *Finsk Tidsskrift för Vitterhet* 92(1922): 123–30.

Ljunggren, G. "Det Moraliske Elementet i Holbergs Komik." *Nordisk Universitets Tidsskrift* 9(1864): 147–81.

———. "Studier öfver Holberg." *Nordisk Universitets Tidsskrift* 9(1864): 26–52.

Logeman, H. "Sproglige Berøringspunkter Mellem Holberg og Ibsen." *Edda* 22(1925): 111–41.

Magnussen, J. "Holberg i Tyskland." *Hjemme og Ude* (1884–85): 113–14.

Martensen, Julius. "Om Holbergs Komedier i de 18 Aar, Da der ikke Gaves Teaterforestillinger i Kjøbenhavn." *Museum* 2(1893): 61–91.

———. "Om Holberg og den Efter Kong Frederik den Femtes Thronbestigelse Gjenoprettede Danske Skueplads." *Museum* 1(1894): 23–56.

———. "Om Teatret i Lille Grønnegade Efter Forestillingen af *Den Danske Komedies Ligbegængelse* og Thaliæ Afskedstale." *Museum* 1(1892): 293–307.

Marker, Frederick J., and Marker, Lise-Lone. *The Scandinavian Theatre: A Short History.* Wallop, Hampshire, England: Basil Blackwell Printers Limited, 1975.

Meyer, Michael. *Ibsen.* Garden City, N.Y.: Doubleday and Company, Inc., 1971.

Molesworth, Robert. *An Account of Denmark as It Was in the Year 1692.* London, 1694.

Moritzen, J. "Holberg and the Danish Stage." *Forum* 68(December 1922): 1026–33.

Müller, Th. A. *Holberg og Danmark.* Copenhagen: Det Berlinske Bogtrykkeri, 1934.

————. "Hvorledes Holberg Blev Baron." *Politiken*, 20 May 1905.

Møller, Christen. *Holbergs Betydning for Dansk Kirkeliv som Komisk Digter*. Copenhagen, 1902.

Neiiendam, Robert. *Det Kongelige Teaters Historie 1874–1890*. 5 vols. Copenhagen, 1921–30. *1890–1892*. Edited by K. Neiiendam. Copenhagen, 1970.

————. "Holberg og Skuepladsen." *Teatret* 9(1909/10): 40.

————. "Holberg og Skuespillerne." *Illustreret Tidende* 64(1922/23): 21–22.

————. *I Memoriam ved Hofteatrets 200 Årsdag d. 30 Januar 1967*. Copenhagen, 1967.

Nielsen, Alfred. "Fortegnelse Over Holbergs Komedier med Angivelse af Første Opførelser." *Boghandlermedhjælperbladet* 1(1884): 80–81.

Nielsen, Harald. *Holberg i Nutidsbelysning*. Copenhagen: H. Aschehoug and Company, 1923.

Nielsen, O. "Nogle Holbergiana." *Litteratur og Kritik* 3(1890): 477–82.

Nielsen, Oluf. *Om København Paa Holbergs Tid*. Copenhagen, 1884.

Nordahl-Olsen, J. *Ludvig Holberg i Bergen, Bidrag til Hans Biografi Paa Grundlag af Nyere Undersøgelser og Arkivstudier*. Bergen, Norway, 1905.

Nyegaard, H. H. "Har Holberg Kendt Shakespeare?" *For Romantik og Historie* 10(1873): 671–80.

Nyrop, Kr. "Holbergiana." *Dania* 10(1903): 129–45.

Nystrøm, Eiler. *Den Danske Komedies Oprindelse: Om Skuepladsen og Holberg*. Copenhagen: Gyldendal, 1918.

Nørbæk, Jens Fr. *Det Holbergske Galleri*. Copenhagen: G. E. C. Gads Forlag, 1967.

Olrik, Hans. "Holberg-litteratur i Anledning af den Danske Skueplads' 200 Aars Jubilæum." *Letterst. tidskrift* (1922): 445–50.

Olsen, B. "Om Kostumering af Holbergske og Molièreske Stykker Paa Det Danske Teater." *Ugeskrift for Theater og Musik* 1(1880): 16–17.

Olsvig, Viljam. *Det Store Vendepunkt i Holbergs Liv.* Copenhagen, 1895.

———. *Nogle Historiske Forstudier til Holbergs Selvbiografi og til Hans Livshistorie.* Copenhagen, 1903.

———. *Om Ludvig Holbergs Saakaldte Selvbiografi.* Copenhagen, 1905.

Overskou, Thomas. "Den Holbergske Comedie Paa den Danske Skueplads til Clementins Død." *Fædrelandet,* 2–7 July 1847.

———. "Sammenligning imellem Holberg og Molière." *Portefeuillen,* 2(Copenhagen, 1840): 50–61.

———. , and Collin, Edgar. *Den Danske Skueplads i Dens Historie fra de Første Spor af Dansk Skuespil Indtil Vor Tid.* 7 vols. Copenhagen, 1854–76.

Paludan, Hans Aage. "Corneille og Holberg i Deres Forhold til Klassicismen." *Holberg Aarbog.* Edited by Francis Bull and Carl S. Petersen. 1(1920): 129–62.

Paludan, Julius. "Holbergs Forhold til det ældre tyske Drama." *Historisk Tidsskrift* 6. R, 2(1889): 1–66.

———. "Om Dramæts Udvikling i Danmark mellem Skolekomedien og Holberg." *Historisk Tidsskrift* 5. R, 2(1880–81): 1–84.

Paulli, R. "Ludvig Holberg, 1684–1934." *American Scandinavian Review* 22(December 1922): 423–29.

Petersen, Johs. "Holbergs—sociale—Komedier." *Frederiksborg Højskoles Aarskift.* Hillerød, Denmark, 1930.

Petersen, N. M. *Bidrag til den Danske Litteraturs Historie.* Vol. 5. Copenhagen, 1858.

Philipsen, C. J. A. "Om Holbergs Betydning i Den Komiske Litteratur." *Journal for Litteratur og Kritik* (Copenhagen, 1844): 65–119.

Philipsen, Chr. F. A. *Den Holbergske Literaturs Historie og Bibliografi.* Copenhagen, 1847.

Rahbek, Knud L. "Brev til Prof. Nyerup Adskillige Holbergiana Vedkommende." Æmner 3(1822).

———. "Holberg og Hans Skuespil Vedkommende." Dansk Minerva 7(1918): 173–84.

———. Holbergs Udvalgte Skrifter: Om Ludvig Holberg som Lystspildigter og om Hans Lystspil. Copenhagen, 1817.

Roos, Carl. "Holberg og Lenz." Danske Studier (1914): 21–28.

Skavlan, Olaf. Holberg som Komedieforfatter: Forbilleder og Eftervirkninger. Kristiania, Norway, 1872.

Skeel, Mogens. Grevens og Friherrens Komedie. Edited by Sophus B. Smith. Copenhagen, 1871.

Smith, C. W. Om Holbergs Levnet og Populäre Skrifter. Copenhagen, 1858.

Spang-Hanssen, Ebbe. Erasmus Montanus og naturvidenskaben. Copenhagen, 1965.

Stender-Petersen, Ad. "Holberg og den Russiske Komedie i det 18de Aarhundrede." Holberg Aarbog. Edited by Frances Bull and Carl S. Petersen. 4(1923): 100–51; 5(1924): 142–87; 6(1925): 93–112.

Stühmann, Christian. "William Bloch og Den Stundesløse." Teatret 9(1909/10).

Tarkiainen, V. "Holberg i Finland." Edda 31(1931): 60–80.

Thrap, D. "Fra Holbergs Skoletid." Historisk Tidsskrift, 2nd series, 2:82.

"Tieck om Holbergs Comedier." Aftenblad, 28 March 1823.

Toppelius, O. A. Ludvig Holbergs Komedier. Thesis, Helsingfors University, Finland, 1856.

Topsøe-Jensen, H. G. "Holberg og den Efter Molièreske Komedie." Holberg Aarbog. Edited by Francis Bull and Carl S. Petersen. 2(1921): 112–43.

Trier, H. "Holberg og Den Danske Skueplads." Danske Studier (1907): 140.

"Undervisning Hvorledes Comoedier Skal Sees." Dansk Minerva 6(1818): 439.

Warburg, Karl. *Holberg i Sverige*. Göteborg, Sweden, 1884.

Welhaven, J. E. *Om Ludvig Holberg*. Christiania, Norway, 1854.

Werlauff, E. C. *Historiske Antegnelser til Ludvig Holbergs Atten Første Lystspil*. Copenhagen, 1858.

———. "Oplysning af Enkelte Træk i Holbergs Skuespil." *Nordisk Tidsskrift* 4(1836): 481–84.

Wiingaard, Jytte. *Teaterkundskab—Iscenesættelse*. Copenhagen: Universitets Forlaget, 1972.

———. *William Bloch og Holberg*. Copenhagen: G. E. C. Gads Forlag, 1966.

Index

Gerald S. Argetsinger, a Professor at the National Technical Institute for the Deaf, a college of the Rochester Institute of Technology, currently works as a developmental education specialist. He also serves as Chairman of the American Theatre Association Program on Drama and Theatre by, with, and for Handicapped Individuals. From 1975 to 1978 he was Chairman of the Experimental Educational Theatre at the Institute. Argetsinger holds a Ph.D. in Theatre from Bowling Green State University. He has written and produced several plays and has published articles on educational theatre and theatre for the handicapped. A part-time professional magician, he has also published extensively on magic.